Women in Madina

Through Tabari's Lens

Layali Rihab Cham

Abstract

This analyzes Abu Ja'far Muhammad ibn Jarir al-Tabari's chronicle (d. 923) *History of Prophets and Kings* using a gender perspective. It focuses on al-Tabari's representation of women during the Madina period, arguing that through such a representation al-Tabari projects his Abbasid gender norms on the women of this period. The thesis focuses on four main subjects in relation to al-Tabari's text: the image of rebellious non-Muslim women, 'A'isha's involvement in the Battle of the Camel, and women as rational and emotional players in the Madina period.

Table of Contents

Chapter One

Introductory Remarks

While the ideal goal of many historians may be to write an unbiased record of historical events, this may be considered an impossible task. As Carl N. Degler argues, "Literally thousands of events occurred in any year of the past yet only a fraction of them get into written history. There is selection in any written history regardless of its fullness or length." [1] In spite of the historian's intent his or her *present mindset* plays a significant role in the constructed historical narratives. Even when no explicit explanation is given regarding the standpoint of the author, it may be argued that the selection of reported events may be used as a key signifier in examining the cultural and political views of the historian.

Understanding the historian's socio-political context is therefore important in order to interpret the historical narrative. Medieval historical narratives were constructed in patriarchal cultures, wherein more importance is assigned to the male public sphere focusing on the achievements and roles of powerful men and their state structures. Thus it is not surprising that such a historical narrative gives less importance to the activities of women in either the private or the public spheres. When women do appear in the historical narrative, they are more often than not represented in their traditional roles such as mothers or wives, and not surprisingly when some elite women overstep their expected

---

[1] Carl N. Degler, "Woman as a Force in History by Mary Beard," *The MIT Press* 103 no. 1 (Winter 1974), 70.

gender roles as women players in the social field, we find an implicit critique of such behavior in the historian's narrative. Thus, while one could assume that women must have had an impact on the historical events of their time; this was often downplayed in the conventional historical narrative.

Although in the case of the historical narrative covering the Muslim community in the seventh century women did have an input in transmitting information about the prophetic period, they were not considered to have had a role in the final codified history that emerged centuries later. In this connection, D.A. Spellberg argues that while some of the initial historical reports may have been transmitted by women, the authors of the written historical accounts have all been men.[2] It was these historians who had the final say in what was to be included in, or excluded from the historical narrative and it was these historians whose works were referenced by the succeeding generations. In exploring these historical accounts modern women historians, like Nabia Abbott, Leila Ahmed, and Barbara Freyer Stowasser, have made attempts to re-examine them from a gender sensitive perspective using a feminine lens to show the ways women are represented in this narrative.

As early as 1942 Nabia Abbott published an article in which she argues that women during the time of the Prophet Muhammad were not as constrained in their movement as commonly believed. Rather these perceived constraints should be seen more as projections of the later cultural interpretations of the historians. To come to this conclusion she compared different historical sources, demonstrating how critical modern

---

[2] D. A. Spellberg, <u>Politics Gender, and the Islamic Past: the Legacy of 'A'isha bint Abi Bakr</u> (New York: Columbia University Press, 1994), 11.

scholarship could expose the gender biases of these conventional historical texts.

Abbott argues that compared to later historical periods, women in the early period appear

to have had relative freedom of movement and were more politically active. She

explains, "that at the very beginning of the period woman enjoyed full religious

liberty…numerous and well authenticated are the cases of women, high or low in station,

who exercised this freedom." [3] She further offers evidence that "women of Madina were

present at the very first definite politico-religious alliance made by Mohammed."[4]

Furthermore Abbott demonstrates that there is evidence of women giving political

pledges prior to the military battles of the Muslim Madina community. [5] Thus she argues

that:

> [Muhammad] had no definite intention of categorically disqualifying all
> women for state service and condemning any or all of their efforts in that
> direction. It is, therefore, highly improbable that he is responsible for any
> or all of the different versions of a tradition accredited to him—a tradition
> that was invoked for the first time in connection with 'A'ishah's leadership
> in the civil war against 'Ali. The story is that when Mohammed, who
> watched with keen interest the fatal struggle between Byzantium and
> Persia, heard that a woman sat on the Persian throne, he made the
> statement that a people who place a woman over their affairs are
> unfortunate or unhappy or do not prosper. It is this statement that is made
> the basis of political discrimination against the Moslem woman. [6]

Leila Ahmed continues Abbott's research in her discussion of the various factors that

impacted on women during the Madina period. She argues that because of the strong

ideological stances that existed during the crystallization of Abbasid Islamic history, the

complexity and diversity of Pre-Islamic Arabia have been ignored. "The subject [of

---

[3] Nabia Abbott, "Women and the State in Early Islam," Journal of Near Eastern Studies 1 no. 1 (Jan., 1942), 107.
[4] Ibid, 116.
[5] Ibid, 117.
[6] Ibid, 120-121.

women] being so ideologically charged it has tended to generate a literature of assertion rather than evidence."[7] She remarks that while previously it has been proposed that Islam improved the status of women, this cannot be applied in general terms. While Islamic teachings did improve the status of women in some respects she argues that it detracted power from others particularly in the realm of marriage. Ahmed further argues that, "There was no single, fixed institution of marriage at the time of the advent of Islam and that a variety of types of union were practiced by both women and men."[8] Qur'anic rules however reduced marriage to a singular more male dominant form rendering all other forms as *zina*, or adultery. While these rules applied to marriage may have improved conditions for some women, Ahmed cautions against the idea that it was an improvement for all women. Although Abbot argues that Islamic history was corrupted in its transmission and Ahmed contends it merely crystallized in a more patriarchal form, both scholars agree that the historical narratives should be re-visited and re-interpreted with a critical view of the patriarchal biases of the historians.

Using earlier textual sources, like the Qur'an, *hadiths* and some early Qur'anic commentary, Barbara Freyer Stowasser argues that one finds a more diverse representation of women in these earlier sources than the ones constructed by later generation historians. Referencing these sources in her book, *Women in the Qur'an, Traditions, and Interpretation*, she argues that Madina's socio-political context did not appear to be as patriarchally circumscribed as the later historical narratives describe it. Stowasser proposes that while the early teachings of Islam sought to raise women's status

---

[7] Leila Ahmed, "Women and the Advent of Islam," *Signs* 11, no. 4 (Summer, 1986), 666.
[8] Ahmed, "Women and the Advent of Islam", 668.

compared to men, as the armies of the Arab Muslim state successfully conquered more complex patriarchal cultures, later historians contemporary to the Abbasid period projected their own reinterpretations of the Madina period and its events. Stowasser further argues that, " Medieval Islamic society was patriarchal to a far higher degree than had been the early Islamic community in Mecca and Medina, first recipients of the Qur'an's revelations…While formulating normative interpretations of the Qur'an's women parables in accordance with existing social norms and values, these scholars' consensus, of need, embraced and canonized preexisting traditions in scripturalist language."[9]

Based on such considerations, I would like to argue that the construction of the image of women in the historical narratives was influenced by the patriarchal cultures of the conquered territories. In this study I would like to explore how male-authored historical accounts are constructed from a patriarchal ideological perspective that rigidly defines the public as male and the private as female, failing to underline the permeability of these spheres, and instead judging the permeability of these gendered spheres as improper to their patriarchal assumptions. The question of whether these accounts are authentic or not, is not the issue here, but rather to what extent the patriarchal perspective of the male historian is superimposed on the historical accounts regarding the status and role of women.

D.A. Spellberg, in her book *Politics, Gender, and the Islamic Past: The Legacy of 'A'isha bint Abi Bakr,* follows this gender sensitive reading. She examines how the

---

[9] Barbara Freyer Stowasser, *Women in the Qur'an, Traditions, and Interpretation,* (Oxford: Oxford University Press, 1994), 23.

image of 'A'isha bint Abi Bakr was constructed by Shi'i and Sunni medieval historians,

comparing a vast number of medieval historians and theologians throughout different

centuries, like Ibn Sa'd, al- Balādhurī , al- Ṭabarī, Ibn Hishām, Ibn 'Abd Rabbihi, and Ibn

Kathīr. She shows how their representation of 'Ā'isha was manipulated as a tool in the

ideological debates between the different Muslim religious, political groups. She

concludes, "In studying 'A'isha, one studies male intellectual history, not a woman's

history, but reflections about the place of a woman, and by extension all women, in

exclusively male assertions about Muslim society."[10]

The aim of my thesis will be similarly based; however I intend to focus on the

historical narrative of one historian and his representation of women in his accounts. One

of the most important historical narratives for the early history of the Arab-Muslim

empire is Abu Djafar Muhammad ibn Djarir ibn Yazīd al-Tabari's chronicle (d. 923)

History of Prophets and Kings.   Al-Tabari is an important figure in Islamic

historiography because he was the first Muslim historian to write a vast universal history

of the Arab Muslim empire. His historical accounts cover the period from the beginning

of creation up to his own time. To accomplish this, he pieced together a plethora of

previous historians' works in addition to the oral accounts that were circulating during his

time. [11]

In his historical work al-Tabari tries to be as broad and inclusive as possible, often

including multiple, conflicting reports of the same occurrence. Nevertheless a selection

process was assumed by al-Tabari in order to construct his narrative. The focus of my

---

[10] Spellberg, 191.

[11] Ghada Osman, "Oral vs. Written Transmission: The case of Tabari and Ibn Sa'd", *Arabica,* 48 no 1
(2001), 65.

thesis will be on this process of historical selection. More specifically, I will be examining the way he 're-presented' women in his narrative and the implications of such a re-presentation on the roles women should or should not play. Al-Tabari's history largely centers on community or state leaders, whether military or political. While some events in his account of Madina do include female leadership, such as 'A'isha bint Abi Bakr in the Battle of the Camel, the assumption of such leadership on her part is usually cast in a negative light. The majority of women who appear in his history are marginalized and often included only because of their relationship to a male figure either through marriage or kinship.

In my thesis I will be examining the period between the birth of the Muslim community in Madina and the death of the fourth caliph, 'Ali ibn Abi Talib. The Madina period occupies a special significance for Muslims in general, and for al-Tabari in particular, because of its historical as well as its normative significance for later Muslim generations. As argued earlier, the accuracy of his historical narrative will not be my focus, but rather how al-Tabari re-presents the images of women in this normative period. In doing so, I will attempt to contextualize al-Tabari's narrative in the patriarchal politics and culture of the High Abbasid period when the Abbasid empire was at its peak of power.

Although al-Tabari seems to have been cautious in distancing his stand from the historical reports he recorded nonetheless, we must look at how his selective process enforced the beliefs and assumptions of his own culture. While many of the early historians, like Ibn Hisham, Ibn S'ad, as well as al-Tabari went into great details depicting the foundational period of Madina and its politics, there are fewer details on

the active and complex roles women may have played in this socio-political context. As

will be shown in the next chapters, women in al-Tabari's history were often represented

in their proper gender roles prescribed for them by the patriarchal system and culture of a

later period. In emphasizing the roles of women as mothers and wives, these historians

are re-enforcing the cultural roles that are assigned to them by the patriarchal culture of

the historian. Further, in doing so, the historian is implicitly saying that men and women

have different gender roles to play, where the man assumes the role of woman's guardian

and protector. The images depicting these Madina women as ideal gender players are

ideologically significant, for it is the Golden Age which the dominant Sunni Muslim

discourse idealized.

While in this paper I will be focusing on al-Tabari's text it must be noted that al-

Tabari is not solely responsible for the views and opinions his works project. Given the

remaining sources it is difficult to ascertain to what extent he edited or intentionally

omitted parts of history. Thus al-Tabari's works should not only be seen as a product of

the his own beliefs, but as a product of the medieval Abbasid culture, as well as the

cultures the texts or stories were transmitted through.

In chapter two I will examine some of the theoretical concepts I will be using to

examine al-Tabari's text. I will define and explain patriarchy, sex, gender, and the sex

gender system. In using these concepts I will provide more detailed explanations as to

why women's roles have often been underplayed in historical accounts, as well as how

they were represented when they do appear in the narrative.

In the third chapter I will provide a general background on al-Tabari's life and his relation to the power structure. Additionally I will outline the major gender assumptions that are prevalent in the Sunni discourse during the Abbasid period, with a particular focus on women's representations. As I will try to demonstrate, such assumptions appear to be a major influence on al-Tabari's narrative.

In the next three chapters I will analyze al-Tabari's historical accounts from four different focal points. After examining the section of al-Tabari's text that dealt with the Madina period I listed all of the instances in which women are mentioned. Almost all of these instances fit into one of the four focal points I created. Thus my fourth chapter will cover the first of these points, in which I will examine the way al-Tabari writes on women who resisted conversion and integration in the emerging Muslim community in Madina. Here I will try to show how al-Tabari as a historian adopts the hegemonic discourse of his political and cultural background, examining why women who resisted such integration are often 're-presented' negatively as *jahili* players, and enemies of the Muslim community. Not surprisingly, as the historian of the Abbasid Empire, al-Tabari wishes to denounce the image of the 'enemies' of the emerging Arab Muslim community. One strategy that he uses to do this is to depict these *jahili* women as aggressive and their men as weak, demonstrating the *jahili* or upside down feature of their gender relationship. For instance in the case of Qurashis who opposed the Prophet Mohammad, al-Tabari selects re-presentations of how these strong Qurashi women abuse and mock their weak Qurashi men. The first part of this chapter will therefore focus on those Qurashi women and men who resisted integration in the Muslim community. The second part will discuss the women who opposed Abū Bakr during the so-called Wars of

Apostasy. After the Madina armies successfully subdued tribal resistance to the centralization of the state, we find no further mention of women's opposition to the Muslim community in al-Tabari's narrative until the Battle of the Camel, which will be discussed in the subsequent chapter. One could argue that through al-Tabari's negative re-presentations of this 'other' *jahili* woman type, he is implicitly constructing the image of her opposite, the ideal Muslim woman, who is represented as modest and respectful of her gender boundaries.

The fifth chapter will focus on the Battle of the Camel. While al-Tabari generally excludes mentioning Muslim women on the battlefield in his reports, this becomes a focal point of his reporting on this battle. This was the first main battle between two conflicting interest groups in the Madina period. Being a Sunni Muslim, al-Tabari was put in the paradoxical position of having to simultaneously blame and respect 'A'isha bint Abī Bakr. Here the contradiction between the ideal and the practical is at play. While the ideal defines women's proper gender role in the domestic space, 'A'isha, favored wife of the Prophet, goes out and plays a crucial role in battling against 'Ali. Like other historians covering this military event, al-Tabari displays conflicting emotions with regards to 'Aisha's role, both respecting her as wife of the Prophet, but disapproving of her role as an active participant in this event. However, instead of expressing his own critical judgment, al-Tabari cleverly uses the critiques of another of the Prophet's wives to demonstrate the error in A'isha's ways, emphasizing in his account the former's deliberate decision not to be involved in war. He also puts a significant amount of blame on the two Companions of the Prophet, Talha ibn'Ubayd Allah and al-Zubayr ibn al-'Awwam, who went to war along with 'A'isha. Numerous times, he reports of people reprimanding these two men for allowing the Prophet's wife to do what they would not allow their own wives to do. It is interesting to note that in al-Tabari's narrative, we find that the two Companions get condemned for this far more than they get condemned for going to war against 'Ali. This reflects the importance of gender politics and dynamics in al-Tabari's narrative, where he emphasizes the responsibility of men to control their women's behavior. Needless to say that exercising such control is an important feature of al-Tabari's definition of masculinity.

Chapter six will focus on how elite Muslim women who attained influence through their derivative roles as wives and family members of powerful men are represented in al-Tabari's account. Here al-Tabari's depictions shows that the most powerful influence these women had seems to be in advising their husbands or sons on the best course of action. The Prophet Muhammad and the Madina caliphs are shown to have taken advice from their wives that proved to be valuable. Although such a 're-presentation' demonstrates that women did participate in the political decision making process and were portrayed as rational actors, such representation still places the woman in a derivative position, for although her advice could be acted on, she was not the acting agent in this political process. Such a historical representation assumes that women are seen to be most effective in their informal role as advisors to their male players.

In the final chapter I will discuss the last focus of al-Tabari's narrative: women as mourners. Given the focus of al-Tabari's history on those historical events in which men are supposed to play the predominant roles, his coverage of historical events shows less interest in the roles women played, however, this is not the case in matters of death and tragedy. Whereas he rarely writes in detail of men's emotional response to tragic events and when he does, it is typically shown to be controlled and rational, this is an area where women are represented as predominant players. I will argue here that in doing so al-Tabari is emphasizing his patriarchal perception of the feminine as emotional, as opposed to his perception of the masculine as rational.

Chapter Two

Gender Categories Used in Analyzing the Historical Narrative

"We make our own knowledge and are constantly remaking it in the terms that history provides, and that in making knowledge we act upon the power relations in our lives."[12] It may be argued that a written history rather than simply revealing the past often tells far more about the culture in which it was written. In this chapter I will demonstrate the ways in which some historians are influenced by their respective cultural perspectives in writing their historical narrative. Thus I am going to argue that the mindset and cultural conditioning of a historian plays a significant part in the way he represents his historical players and events. While the specific details of the cultural context in which al-Tabari composed his history will be addressed in the next chapter, the present one will outline the analytical tools I will use to examine his cultural context as well as his historical narrative. A gender perspective will be used in order to examine how and when he represents women in his text.

Sex versus Gender

From a gender viewpoint one of the most important points to understand is the conceptual difference between sex and gender. Sex is said to be the "biological distinction " between women and men, [13] which is something that is determined by nature

---

[12] Judith Newton, "Making-and Remaking-History: Another Look at 'Patriarchy'," *Tulsa Studies in Women's Literature* 3 no. 1 (1984): 125.

[13] Gerda Lerner, *The Creation of Patriarchy,* (New York: Oxford University Press, 1986), 238.

and cannot be altered. Thus, genetic characteristics and the fact that women are child-

bearers are attributes of the feminine sex. Hence it is argued, that regardless of how a

woman is socialized she will carry these traits. Gender, on the other hand, is "a religious

and cultural construction, including prescribed, proscribed, and suggested behaviors

relating to women and/or men."[14]

Thus while sex may be a permanent fixture, gender roles can vary vastly

depending on the culture and society in which they are constructed.[15] For instance,

women are naturally the sex that gives birth to children; however, their role as primary

caretakers is defined by cultural norms and is therefore part of gender socialization not

their sex. The anthropologist Gayle Rubin coined the phrase "the sex-gender system" to

help analyze cultures using this framework. This term is used to study the defined roles

imposed on sex because of its gender. The sex-gender system, more specifically, is "the

institutionalized system which allots resources, property, and privileges to persons

according to culturally defined gender roles."[16]

For most traditional thinkers, however, the line between sex and gender is often

blurred in their arguments. The role of the mother as the caretaker and the father as the

provider, they argue, reoccur so often in societies simply because they are a fundamental

part of man's and woman's nature. Anthropologists focusing on a gender perspective,

however, have proven that these are not universal characteristics and consequently are

---

[14] Margot Badran, "Gender" *Encyclopaedia of the Qur'ān*, ed: Jane Dammen McAuliffe, Georgetown University, Washington DC. Brill, 2008. Brill Online, The American University in Cairo <http://0-www.brillonline.nl.lib.aucegypt.edu:80/subscriber/entry?entry=q3_SIM-00167>, par 1.

[15] Gerda Lerner, *The Majority Finds its Past* (New York: The University of North Carolina Press, 1979), 169.

[16] Lerner, *The Creation of Patriarchy*, 238.

not a natural development or an essential nature of one's sex.[17] Nevertheless whether

they are believed to be due to nature or not, it is useful to examine how gender roles, once

defined, inform social behavior and interactions.

The study of gender roles has been a focal point in feminist and gender theories

for decades. Some feminists argue that the insistence on fixed and separate gender roles

is the very cause of male domination in society. Still others argue that separate gender

roles do not necessarily dictate inequality if social norms uphold a "separate but equal"

identity. Historically, however, societies have never been able to uphold this standard of

equality.[18] Once one sex defines itself in negation to the other, it begins to inform the

power structure. If one sex defines itself as superior, it must in turn define the other sex

as inferior. If one sex defines itself as strong, it must in turn define the other sex as weak.

The reason a separation in gender roles tends to eventually create domination of

one gender over the other is explained by Sandra Harding's theory of the "self-other

dichotomy". Men's "search for a separate identity leads them to form rigid ego

boundaries and to tend to regard other persons, especially women, in antagonistic

opposition to themselves. This self-other dichotomy is not merely an opposition, but a

hierarchy in which the self is of greater value. Men thus have a psychic interest in

dominating…Since men design and control all of society's institutions…these institutions

reflect this psychology of self-other domination." [19]

---

[17] Joan Kelly-Gadol, "The Social Relation of the Sexes: Methodological Implications of Women's
   History," *Chicago Journals* 1 no. 4 (Summer, 1976): 815.
[18] Iris Marion Young, "Is Male Gender Identity the Cause of Male Domination?" in *Feminist Social
   Thought*, ed by: Diana Tietjens Meyers (New York: Routledge, 1997), 26.
[19] Young, 26.

Nancy Chodorow also examines the path cultures have taken to prescribe male domination. She argues that the mother's exclusive role in raising children continually reinforces male domination in a society. The mother, because of her own gender identity, treats her daughter as an extension of herself, more so than her son. Therefore the son is taught to think of himself as a separate identity "not merely of defining himself as a different person, but a different kind of person" from his mother.[20] He thus defines his gender in opposition to his mother, and in order to fulfill this prescribed gender role, he seeks to dominate the opposite gender.[21]

Thus the domination of women is influenced by an idealized and unattainable construction of separate and unequal gender roles. Moreover, the continual renewal of these idealized roles needs to be supported by culture at least at the normative level. Judith Butler argues that "the body' itself [is] shaped by political forces with strategic interest in keeping that body bounded and constituted by the marker of sex."[22] This 'political force' is often embodied in a culture that continually tries to restrict the woman from acting outside of her defined gender role. Culture can do this in many ways, through laws, institutions, religion, and, most importantly to my thesis, in the writing of historical narrative.

The inscribing of history may play a significant part in maintaining fixed gender identities and upholding a restricting frame of possibilities and performances, both necessary to the construction of male domination. As Butler argues, "Gender reality

---

[20] Young, 23.

[21] Young, 25.

[22] Judith Butler, "Excerpt from Gender Trouble," in *Feminist Social Thought,* ed by: Diana Tietjens Meyers (New York: Routledge, 1997), 113.

created through sustained social performances means that the very notions of an essential sex and a true or abiding masculinity or femininity are also constituted as part of the strategy that conceals gender's performative character and the performative possibilities for proliferating gender configuration outside the restricting frame of masculinist domination."[23] In writing a history informed by one's cultural gender norms, these norms are perceived as a permanent fixture of human nature, denying, as Butler argues the significance of social interaction and performativity as an alternative view to examine the different variety of practices of gender roles. Thus if the historian inscribes the normative gender roles of women as simply mothers, wives, or daughters, women would regard this to be their normal roles in society.

Patriarchy

The sex-gender or patriarchal framework is important to reference in analyzing historical texts, and it is also useful in understanding the power structure of the society in which such texts are composed. Historically, the patriarchal ideological structure has informed the social interaction between men and women. While this structure has developed in many forms, the most fundamental characteristic of it is that the men are assigned a dominant position of authority and power in relation to women. Further patriarchy "implies that men hold power in all the important institutions of society and that women are deprived of access to such power." [24]

---

[23] Butler, 122.
[24] Lerner, *The Creation of Patriarchy,* 239.

A discursive division between the private and public spheres of life is a common feature in patriarchal discourses. Even though men, as well as, women appear as actors in both social spheres, in patriarchal discourses women's primary location are usually assigned to the private or domestic sphere. Moreover, within this sphere they are traditionally viewed as the subordinate actors. This discursive division in spheres continues to perpetuate the domination of men, as Chodorow explains:

> [When] women's primary location [is] in the domestic sphere [this]
> creates a basis for the structural differentiation of domestic and public
> spheres. But these spheres operate hierarchically. Kinship rules organize
> claims of men on domestic units, and men dominate kinship. Culturally
> and politically, the public sphere dominates, and hence men dominate
> women.[25]

Although in the patriarchal structure women may hold less power in either sphere, this does not mean that they lack agency in social performative interactions. Lerner argues that patriarchy "does not imply that women are either totally powerless or totally deprived of rights, influences, and resources."[26] Although the ways women use their agency may vary in different patriarchal contexts, they seem to be constantly negotiating relations of power existing in their society to their interest. As is evidently demonstrated in historical narratives, women were not pure victims throughout history, and although traditional history would like to assign them an agency constrained by their normative gender role, the very same narrative often demonstrates how women manipulated the social and political structures of their society to their advantage. A case in point here is 'A'isha; even though al-Tabari's narrative is critical of her transgression of gender boundaries by actively participating in a military battle, it cannot be denied that she

---

[25] Young, 24
[26] Lerner, *The Creation of Patriarchy,* 239.

played a major role in the political conflicts of the Madina period, actively seeking political alliances to strengthen her own position in these conflicts.

Lerner's analysis of patriarchy provides a ground for modern historians to revisit traditional history from a gender sensitive perspective, demonstrating that women were not as absent as some historians would like us to believe. Women did exercise different forms of power and influence throughout time, although constrained by a prescribed and more restrictive gender role in relation to men. As Lerner comments, "Common-sense observation and reasoning tell us that half of the world's work, half of the world's experiences, has been [women's]. And yet in recorded history, authored by male historians, women appear only as marginal contributors to human development."[27] These critical comments will be dealt with in the next section in examining the reasons why women are represented in al-Tabari's history in marginal roles.

Marginalizing Women in History

Even though women sometimes appear in historical texts, they are usually represented in marginal roles. Some modern defenders of traditional history tend to argue why this is the case. Historian J. H. Hexter articulates this point in his essay in the *New York Times,* when confronting feminist historian Mary Beard. He states that the reason women do not take up half of the figures in history is because the main focus of

---

[27] Lerner, *The Majority Finds its Past,* 169.

history is with the process of change over time. "We know who was mainly behind those trends and developments and movements. For better or worse, it was men."[28]

Women historians contend with this argument in different ways. First it is argued that women were indeed involved in the changes that occurred, but male-authored narratives do not document the roles they played. This is not necessarily done out of malice, but may be considered as an oversight by the historians as a result of their gender conditioning. The works of Beard largely support this view. In her works she shows the misconceptions of widely respected male historians in the way they represented women in modern Western society. In examining differing texts of Western history, in her works she points out the important events in which women participated, but which were ignored by the historian. Although some primary sources documented the role of women in these events, modern historians only focused on the roles of the men. She argues that by simply not asking what roles women played in history, women were represented as unimportant actors, whether they had a role in altering events or not.

While the modern historians Beard first reviewed were largely isolated from women in the academic field, she later proves how this pattern continued even after women became members of the academy. Beard examined the works of John Spencer Bassett who wrote on the state of Western society in the eighteenth century. Despite the fact that he had been teaching for years at Smith College for women, there was a complete absence of women in his historical studies.[29] Beard's argument creates a strong case for the fact that even though women have been involved in historical events, their

---

[28] Degler, 73.
[29] Degler, 69.

roles were simply ignored by historians who were not informed by a gender sensitive perspective.

Another theory explaining the absence of women in history can further be derived from Hexter's article. While he argues that historians often only look to sources of changes, he fails to articulate the type of change they look for.[30] Although male-centered change is often the focus of historians, one must note the many different types of changes, which largely are ignored by historians. Joan Kelly-Gadol also explains "Throughout historical times, women have been largely excluded from making war, wealth, laws, governments, art, and science. Men, functioning in their capacity as historians, considered exactly those activities to be constitutive of civilization: hence, diplomatic history, economic history, constitutional history, and political and cultural history."[31]

Similarly, Learner argues, "patriarchal values dominate and order the writing of history. It is assumed that 'man is the measure of significance' so that the activities of men are seen as being interesting, more significant than the activities of women."[32] Thus one could argue that it is the male-centered mindset of historians that is one of the reasons behind the relative absence of women in historical writing. Some women historians also suggest that historians should focus on other sources of change allowing

---

[30] Degler, 73.
[31] Kelly-Gadol, 811.
[32] Lerner, *The Majority Finds its Past*, 169.

new actors to come to light. For instance, if historians used turning points revolving

around childbirth, sexuality, or family structure a new type of history would emerge.[33]

Although one way to de-marginalize women may be to change the focus of the

historical narrative, it is not practical to abandon traditional history altogether, for it tells

an important part of the past. Even if the focus may contribute to a relative absence of

female agency, it should be adapted or revisited in order to integrate a gender dynamics

framework. Beard suggests that even if we continue to use the male-centered spheres in

history, if we use less focus on individualized events, a fuller picture of history may come

forth. Hence instead of focusing solely on a leader more attention could be placed on the

family context in which both men and women functioned.[34] Furthermore, whether or not

women were directly involved in the choices of diplomacy, war, or law, there is historical

evidence that shows how they had influence on the male players with whom they were

directly associated.

This is not only true of European social history, but it is true of Abbasid history as

well. One has to just read Abbott's pioneering study of the decisive roles the mothers

and wives of Abbasid caliphs played in the politics of their time. In her study Abbott

details the lives and vast influences of two of the Abbasid Empire's most influential

women, Khaizurān and Zubaidah. Khaizuran, for example, was not only able to secure

both of her sons' places in succession for the caliphate, during her second son's rule she

was able to act with control or at lest influence over many governmental decisions. "[The

caliph] allowed her a free hand and, at times, restrained his own desires out of deference

---

[33] Kelly-Gadol, 812.
[34] Degler, 72.

to her expressed wishes…Khaizuran shared power with the grand wazir, who, for as long as she lived, consulted her on all state and palace affairs."[35] Thus Khaizuran, Abbott shows, was able to not only be a source of information as an advisor, as al-Tabari writes the women of Medina to have been, but she was able to have direct influence in the public realm and at times act as a ruler.

As Lerner points out, women may have been economically, educationally, legally, and opportunity wise oppressed like other minorities, nevertheless women cannot be regarded as a monolithic group, for they belonged to different socio-economic classes and races.[36] For instance, women who belonged to the powerful elite class, unlike poor women, usually exercised influential roles and had much to say in the politics and economy of their society. Once again, it can be argued that in the Madina period the wives and daughters of Caliphs and important Companions had influential roles to play, in spite of their gender restraints.

Gender historians have often demonstrated how the notion of the strong woman conflicts with the ideal image of woman as defined by a patriarchal culture. Despite the gap between the ideal image of woman and the actual roles she played, there has been constant negotiation between both.[37] As Carl N. Degler rightly argues there is a "tendency to confuse prescriptive literature with actual behavior. In fact, what we are learning from most of these monographs is not what women, did, felt, or experienced, but

---

[35] Nabia Abbott, *Two Queens of Bagdad, Mother and Wife of Harun al-Rashid* (Chicago: University of Chicago Press, 1946), 114.
[36] Lerner, *The Majority Finds its Past*, 170.
[37] Ibid, 12.

what men in the past thought women should do."[38] Consequently when examining

historical writing that is informed by patriarchal thinking it is important to examine it

through a critical lens, and with a view on the ways it represents the role women played

in a specific historical context. Like other male historians discussed above, al-Tabari

focuses on the actions of men rather than those of women. This is not to insinuate that

his history of the Madina period is inaccurate, merely that it is presented and composed

from material and thought of a patriarchal framework. Thus we must pay special

attention to how women, when they do appear, are represented in his narrative, and how

he sees their roles and actions through the patriarchal lens of his cultural background.

---

[38] Lerner, *The Majority Finds its Past*, 148.

Chapter Three

The Representation of Women in Sunni Abbasid Discourse

The influence of one's culture and beliefs often plays an important role in the historical curiosity one exhibits and the narratives they produce. Sunni discourse of the Abbasid era typically idealizes the first generation of Muslim believers. Not only is the prophetic period regarded as one that achieved unity and justice for the Muslim community, but this discourse also regarded the *sahabi* period of Madina to be one that followed closely in the footsteps of the Prophet's path, thus representing that period as the Rightly Guided Caliphate. In matters relating to gender, it is argued here that historians such as al-Tabari have projected the patriarchal values of their own era unto the Madina period, which they then constructed as the golden age that Muslims should look up to. As Gerda Lerner argues, "As long as androcentric assumptions dominated our interpretations, we read the sex/gender arrangements prevailing in the present backward into the past. We assumed the existence of male dominance as a given and considered any evidence to the contrary merely an exception to the rule or a failed alternative."[39]

In this chapter, I will make an attempt to depict the cultural background of al-Tabari's Abbasid era, in order to demonstrate in the following chapters, as Lerner's statement indicates, that his androcentric values are projected onto his representation of women of the Madina period through his narrative. As we shall see, al-Tabari's historical

---

[39] Lerner, *The Creation of Patriarchy, 15-16.*

accounts underplayed the role of women in the recording of this period. However,

when women are represented, it is usually either to celebrate their 'proper' feminine role,

or to condemn them for transgressing their role's boundaries.

Al-Tabari's Background and his Relationship to the Abbasid Caliphate

While it is important to examine al-Tabari's biographical background for the

purposes of analyzing his text, little is actually known about his life. There are no

primary biographical sources on him, and all of the current information we have was

recorded or indeed written during this period, composed by later scholars. Al-Tabari was

born around 225AH/839CE, and lived until the age of twelve in Tabaristan. This was

during the reign of the caliph al-Mu'tasim (d.227AH/842CE), which was a century of

intellectual renaissance and debate, as well as political upheavals. Many of the canonical

texts of Arab and Muslim scholarship were recorded in this period, including works by

Ash'ari (d. 324AH/935-6CE) and Ibn Hanbal (d. 241AH/855CE) to mention but a few.[40]

Al-Tabari came from a family of financial stability and was thus able to study and travel

extensively as a student.[41] After attending lectures and studying in Persia, Syria,

Palestine, and Egypt he finally settled in Baghdad in 256AH/870CE. He continued to

live there for his final fifty years, teaching and writing in multiple fields of religious and

historical scholarship.[42]

---

[40] C.E. Bosworth, "al- Tabari, Abū Dj'afar Muhammad b. Djarir b. Yazid," *Encyclopaedia of Islam, Second Edition*, ed by P. Bearman et all. Brill, 2009 Brill Online, American University in Cairo, 25 February 2009 <http://0-www.brillonline.nl.lib.aucegypt.edu/subscriber/entry?entry=islam_COM-1133>, par 10.
[41] Bosworth, par 2-3.
[42] Bosworth, par 6-7.

During his stay in Baghdad al-Tabari was prolific in his writing. One story

states that he wrote forty pages a day for forty years.[43] The works that he is most highly

known for are his universal history and his Qur'anic *tafsir*. In these works he used the

practice of *ijtihād*, the independent exercise of judgment, to interpret his sources. While

all of his texts were founded on other written works and reports that existed in his time,

he was able to exercise authorship by selecting the report he believed to be the most

acceptable.[44]

In his writings one can detect strong Orthodox Sunni tendencies.[45] The general

principles for Sunni discourse in the Abbasid era, firstly, were in support of state power

and its role in guiding Islamic values and ensuring the unity of the community. Ira M.

Lapidus argues, "The effort to bring Muslim religious life under state supervision

descended from both Byzantine and Sassanian conceptions of the proper relationship

between the state and religion."[46] Thus it is not surprising that this view, at that time,

conflicted with other views of Islamic political thought. Additionally Sunni doctrine

tends to give strong support to all four of the Rightly Guided Caliphs.[47] This Sunni frame

of mind and its implications on gender thought will be discussed further in the next

section.

Al-Tabari's relation to the power structure of the Abbasid Empire is hard to

---

[43] Devin J. Stewart, "Muhammad b. Jarir al-Tabari's al-Bayan 'an Usul al-Ahkam and the Genre of Usul al Fiqh in Ninth Century Baghdad," in *Abbasid Studies: Occasional Papers of the School of 'Abbasid Studies Cambridge 6-10 July 2002*, ed by: James E. Montgomery (Dudley: Peeters Publishers & Department of Oriental Studies Bondgenotenlaan, 2004), 327.

[44] Bosworth, par 13.

[45] Bosworth, par 10.

[46] Ira M. Lapidus, *A History of Islamic Societies* (New York: Cambridge University Press, 1988), 88.

[47] Bosworth, par 10.

determine. He was able to primarily finance himself using his inherited estate, which

was left to him by his family in Tabaristan.[48] According to most sources, despite the fact

that al-Tabari was well suited to be either a court historian or a judge, the Abbasid caliphs

did not patronize al-Tabari's works.[49] The closest he ever came to being financially

connected to the caliphate was in tutoring the son of al-Mutawakkil's vizier, however,

this position only lasted for a few years.[50] According to Lapidus, al-Tabari was

considered part of the religious elite. He argues that within Abbasid doctrine there were

two parties that exerted input on the Islamic faith: the imperial elite and the religious

elite. "Officially, the Muslim community was headed by the Caliph and his governors,

but in fact the learned and pious people who held no official position, but who had

acquired a reputation for knowledge and devotion to the faith, were accepted by ordinary

Muslims as the true authorities on Islam. These devotees of Islam formed circles of

disciples and students."[51] Yet even though al-Tabari was not connected to the Abbasid

state, he was ideologically acting, according to what Claude Cahen calls a "loyal subject"

of the state, supporting the same Orthodox Sunni ideology. While in his works al-Tabari

sometimes used sources that may be considered outside of the accepted Sunni Abbasid

discourse, he did this only when they did not contradict his Sunni ideological

framework.[52] Thus, within his scholarship we find a firm support of the Sunni Abbasid

culture and its hegemony over other ideological frameworks that existed during that

---

[48] Hugh Kennedy, *When Baghdad Ruled the Muslim World: The Rise and Fall of Islam's Greatest Dynasty* (Cambridge: Da Capo Press, 2004), xxi.

[49] Bosworth, par 7

[50] Bosworth, par 4.

[51] Lapidus, 99.

[52] Claude Cahen, "History and Historians," in *Religion, Learning and Science in the 'Abbasid Period,* ed by M.J.L. Young, J.D. Latham and R.B. Serjeant (Cambridge: Cambridge University Press, 1990), 200.

period.

In al-Tabari's narrative of the Madina period, it is argued that one finds that women are represented in a much more conservative, restricted manner than what modern historians suggest to have actually happened during that period. Given the lapse of over two hundred years between the Madina period and its recording by al-Tabari, some historians argue there were major shifts in cultural norms, as Byzantine and Sassanian norms seem to have been absorbed into what came to be regarded as the normative Muslim culture.[53] After the death of the fourth caliph of Madina the capital of the Arab Muslim state moved to Syria and later Baghdad, where sedentary environments and more complex cultures developed, and where views on women's roles seem to have been more rigidly defined.[54] In this connection, Leila Ahmed argues:

> The practices sanctioned by Muhammad within the first Muslim society
> were enunciated in the context of far more positive attitudes toward
> women than the later Abbasid society was to have…the social context in
> which the textual edifice was created was far more negative for women
> than that in Arabia, so the spiritually egalitarian voice of the religion
> would have been exceedingly difficult to hear…Such practices, and the
> conceptions [the Abbasid era] gave rise to, informed the dominant
> ideology and affected how Islam was heard and interpreted in this period
> and how its ideas were rendered into law.[55]

For instance, while restrictions on women's movement were less practiced in the tribal culture of Arabia, it was an established cultural norm in the Byzantine and Sassanian cultural environments. In Byzantine culture, "proper conduct for girls entailed that they be neither heard nor seen outside of their home. Women were not supposed to be seen in

---

[53] Reuben Levy, *The Social Structure of Islam: Being the Second Edition of the Sociology of Islam*
   (Cambridge: University Press, 1957), 130.
[54] Ahmed, *Women and Gender: Historical Roots of a Modern Debate*, 26.
[55] Ibid, 67.

public. Women were always supposed to be veiled, the veil or its absence marking the

distinction between 'honest' women and the prostitute."[56] Ahmed further argues that

during the Abbasid period the dominant Muslim discourse came to identify itself more

closely with Judaism and Christianity, and it was able to adopt many of the misogynistic

tendencies that the Byzantine and Sassanian cultures left behind. This included the

Christian notion of the shamefulness of sex, particularly focused on the female body.[57]

Women, particularly those who belonged to the 'respectable' classes, were hence to be

hidden from the sight of men so as to avoid the possibility of sinful acts. Ahmed also

argues that while rules restricting the movement and appearance of women may have

been present in the Qur'an, such as the restrictive verses regarding the Prophet's wives

these were meant to protect his wives from the intrusion of non-believers.[58] Furthermore,

such rules did not seem to apply to all women, for class seems to be an important factor

determining the degree of restrictions imposed on women's movement.

The Abbasid notions on gender, as Ahmed contends, were not universal within

the Abbasid Empire; rather they stood in contrast to surrounding minority religious sects:

> From the beginning there were those who emphasized the ethical and
> spiritual message as the fundamental message of Islam and argued that the
> regulations Muhammad put into effect, even his own practices, were
> merely the ephemeral aspects of the religion, relating only to that
> particular society at that historical moment. Thus they were never
> intended to be normative or permanently binding for the Muslim
> community. Among the groups that to some degree or other took this
> position were the Sufis, the Kharijis, and the Qarmatians
> (Qaramita)…However, throughout history it has not been those who have
> emphasized the ethical and spiritual dimensions of the religion who have

---

[56] Ahmed, *Women and Gender: Historical Roots of a Modern Debate,* 26.
[57] Ibid, 36.
[58] Ibid, 55.

held power. The political, religious, and legal authorities in the Abbasid period in particular, whose interpretative and legal legacy has defined Islam ever since, heard only the androcentric voice of Islam, and they interpreted the religion as intending to institute androcentric laws and an androcentric vision in all Muslim societies throughout time.[59]

Given the factional debates within the Abbasid cultural context during al-Tabari's time, it could be argued that he tried to distance himself and his ideas from those of the oppositional groups, and in turn their more egalitarian notions on gender. Thus within the composition of his history one can see how he could try to set or confirm the normative gender thought of his time. For the use of history can be a powerful tool in setting and conforming gender norms. As Lerner argues:

> Most significant of all the impediments toward developing group consciousness for women was the absence of a tradition which would reaffirm the independence and autonomy of women at any period in the past. There had never been any woman or group of women who had lived without male protection, as far as most women knew. There had never been any group of persons like them who had done anything significant for themselves. Women had no history—so they were told; so they believed. Thus, ultimately, it was men's hegemony over the symbol system which most decisively disadvantaged women.[60]

While there was a shift in culture between the Madina and later the Abbasid periods, a true history of the Madina period is hard to attain. Given that the sources we have of the Madina period, with the exception of the Qur'an, were recorded in the Abbasid period or thereafter, my analysis of al-Tabari's historical narrative will therefore underline how al-Tabari's representation of women from the Madina period was necessarily influenced by his own patriarchal perspective of gender roles in the cultural context in which he lived.

It is important to re-note that much of his works is not solely a product of his own labor,

---

[59] Ahmed, *Women and Gender: Historical Roots of a Modern Debate,* 66.
[60] Lerner, *The Creation of Patriarchy,* 219.

but is influenced by the culture it arouse in. While Abbasid gender discourse cannot be said to be static or resistant to changes over time, one can point to some of its general features, which needless to say, were commonly assumed by other patriarchal cultures from different historical periods.

As Lerner argues one of the most effective forces for male domination was the male monopoly on definitions.[61] Although the actual gender practices of Abbasid culture may not have completely adhered to these ideal patriarchal definitions they represented the hegemonic Abbasid gender model. In examining this hegemonic gender discourse I will be highlighting three significant features: the argument for the innate differences between the sexes; the reason for male dominance of women; and justification of women's exclusion from the public sphere. In the following chapters I will show how these points of gender discrimination are constantly referenced in al-Tabari's narrative.

Gender Relations in Sunni Abbasid Discourse

Early Sunni scholars of the Abbasid era sought to justify and legitimize their cultural discourse through use of an Islamic language. Given that the Qur'an was relatively brief on matters of detail in gender relations, later generations of Sunni scholars used the *hadith* as a primary source of reference in constructing gender roles according to Islamic teachings and ethics. Scholars such as Schacht, Goldziher, and others argue that many of the *hadith*s concerning the construction of gender roles seem to have originated not in seventh century Madina, but closer to the period when they were codified, i.e. in

---

[61] Lerner, *The Creation of Patriarchy,* 220.

the eighth or ninth century.[62] As Barbara Stowasser points out:

> Within the newly expanded realm of Islam, later generations of Muslims,
> most of them not of Arab stock, came to see the Prophet in terms of a
> personal infallibility and sinlessness that had not been perceived in
> contemporaries in Mecca and Medina. The Hadith is both a record of
> what Muhammad actually said and did and also a record of what his
> community in the first two centuries of Islamic history believed that he
> said and did. Thus the Hadith has been called 'a guide to understanding
> the historical Muhammad as well as a guide to understanding the
> evolution of Muslim piety from the seventh to the ninth centuries.' Even
> in the authenticated Hadith, 'history' and 'example' were intertwined in
> the compilers' intent and methodology were not to record historical dater
> per se but to institutionalize Muhammad's exemplary behavior for the
> benefit of the community.[63]

Thus the Islamic ideas that developed as the Empire grew and moved over the ruins of

the Byzantine culture can be seen more strongly in the *hadiths*. The first of these ideas,

which was prevalent in the Abbasid era, is the patriarchal assumption of the innate

difference between the masculine and feminine, which in turn justifies different gender

roles for men and women. Such a belief is assumed by other patriarchal societies, as

Lerner comments, "Traditionalists accept the phenomenon of 'sexual asymmetry,' the

assignment of different tasks and roles to men and women, which has been observed in

all known human societies, as proof of their position and evidence of its 'naturalness.'

Since woman was, by divine design assigned a different biological function than man,

they argue, she should also be assigned different social tasks."[64] While one can see how

this assumption was constructed and legitimized in the *hadith* narrative codified in the

Abbasid period, it is mainly absent in the Qur'an, or at least not explicitly stated as it is in

---

[62] Joseph Schacht, "A Revaluation of Islamic Traditions," in *Hadith: Origins and Development,* ed by
Harald Motzki (Burlington, Vermont: Ashgate-Variorum 2001).
[63] Stowasser, *Women in the Qur'an, Traditions, and Interpretation,* 104.
[64] Lerner, *The Creation of Patriarchy,* 16.

the *hadiths*.

The Qur'anic text is regarded largely as a spiritual document, which does not define in detail distinct gender roles for men and women, nevertheless brief allusions to such roles can be found within it. For instance, in the Qur'an it is plainly stated that, "the male is not like the female."[65] Taken at face value, the former statement simply states that there is a difference between the male and female, but it does not elaborate further privileging one gender over the other. However, in analyzing the Qu'ranic text Margot Badran argues that there are strong notions of gender roles represented within it, where women are often described as the caretakers and are most frequently only mentioned in relation to men—mainly as wives.[66] Still, while these differences may be inferred from the Qur'anic narrative, Muslim scholars needed to interpret and elaborate on such references in constructing their cultural notions of gender difference, where masculinity appears to have a more privileged role than femininity.

Therefore more so than the Qur'an, the Sunni *hadith* narrative, which came to be codified in the early Abbasid era, played a more important role in the Islamization of the already existing cultural norms of that period. Such *hadith* narrative, in contrast to the Qur'an, was more prone to fabrication and elaboration on the part of its scholars and transmitters. Studies of the *hadiths* of the Prophet and his Companions have shown that there is clearly a more negative tone towards women and a stricter definition of their role

---

[65] *Qur'an*, trans by Ahmed Ali (Princeton: Princeton University Press, 1984), Verse 3:36.

[66] Margot Badran, "Gender," *Encyclopaedia of the Qur'ān*, ed by: Jane Dammen McAuliffe, Georgetown University, Washington DC. Brill, 2008, Brill Online, American University in Cairo, 23 October 2008 <http://0-www.brillonline.nl.lib.aucegypt.edu:80/subscriber/entry?entry=q3_SIM-00167>, par 2.

within them.[67] For example, in one *hadith* the Prophet describes the different roles a

woman should play in order to please God. According to this *hadith* it is stated that

women who are "child-bearers, mothers, nurses who are compassionate toward their

children, and those who pray will enter Paradise, provided that they do not commit

wrongs against their husbands."[68]

Not only does this *hadith* define the proper roles women should perform, but it

stipulates a condition: paradise is only for those women who obey and therefore please

their husbands. As Lerner argues, "The traditionalist explanation focuses on woman's

reproductive capacity and sees in motherhood woman's chief goal in life, by implication

defining as deviant women who do not become mothers."[69] In addition to defining the

roles women should play, the *hadiths* also help in justifying why they should play these

roles by reaffirming the innate differences between men and women. In one *hadith* Ali

ibn Abi Talib, the fourth caliph is supposed to have said:

> The worst characteristics of men constitute the best characteristics of
> women; namely stinginess, pride, and cowardice for if the woman is
> stingy, she will preserve her own and her husband's possession; if she is
> proud she will refrain from addressing loose and improper words to
> everyone; and if she is cowardly, she will dread everything and will
> therefore not go out of her house and will avoid compromising situations
> for fear of her husband. These accounts indicate the sum total of the good
> qualities sought in marriage.[70]

It is not surprising that as these *hadiths* grew in popularity these innate gender differences

were interpreted within Sunni discourse as God privileging one sex over the other. As

---

[67] Stowasser, *Women in the Qur'an, Traditions, and Interpretation,* 105-106.

[68] Al-Ghazali, *Marriage and Sexuality in Islam,* trans by Madelain Farah (Salt Lake City: University of
Utah Press, 1984), 121.

[69] Lerner, *The Creation of Patriarchy,* 17.

[70] Al-Ghazali, 85-6.

was argued in the previous chapter, stricter gender roles often justify greater inequality between the sexes; we can therefore see how this argument for innate difference is often used to justify male domination over women. While such argument for domination may be inferred from some Qur'anic verses, it is more reasonable to argue that it finds its legitimacy in the *hadiths* and *tafsir* literature. One may even argue that the Qur'an in many places actually contradicts this theme of inequality, setting forth an ideal of equality between the sexes:

> For Muslim men and women, for believing men and women, for devout
> men and women, for truthful men and women, for men and women who
> are patient and constant, for men and women who humble themselves, for
> men and women who give in charity, for men and women who fast, for
> men and women who guard their chastity, and for men and women who
> engage much in Allah's praise, for them has Allah prepared forgiveness
> and great reward.[71]

On this verse Ahmed comments, "Balancing virtues and ethical qualities, as well as concomitant reward, in one sex with the precisely identical virtues and qualities in the other, the passage makes a clear statement about the absolute identity of the human moral condition and the common and identical spiritual and moral obligations placed on all individuals regardless of sex."[72]

The second concept of the necessity of male domination may be illustrated in several popular *hadiths* from the Abbasid period. In one *hadiths,* for example, the Prophet is reported to have said, "Marriage is enslavement; let one therefore be careful in whose hands he places his daughter. Exercising caution on her behalf is important, because she becomes a slave by the marriage and cannot be freed from it, while the

---

[71] Verse 33:35.
[72] Ahmed, *Women and Gender: Historical Roots of a Modern Debate*, 65.

husband is able to obtain divorce at all times."[73] In this *hadith*, there is no expectation

of equality, but for a marriage to function properly a wife must obey her husband almost

in a slave like fashion. Further according to this *hadith* the woman is not only expected

to be obedient to her husband, but to her father as well, and seemingly lacking any choice

or independence of her own.

We should take into account, however, that such patriarchal discourse attributed

to the Prophet was not necessarily followed by women in practice. For if women did not

in practice contest such discourses of obedience there would not be such a proliferation of

these obedience *hadiths* circulating during the Abbasid period. An examination of al-

Tabari's historical narrative of Madina will demonstrate for instance that women such as

'Aisha did not follow such restrictive patriarchal rules.

The notion of male domination in the Sunni discourse can further be seen through

some of the medieval *tafsir* literature. Al-Ghazali (d. 1111) one of the most notable

medieval Sunni theologians who crystallizes later Abbasid thought, tells us:

> Allah has preferred the one sex over the other in the matter of mental
> ability and good counsel, and in their power for the performance of duties
> and for carrying out of [divine] commands. Hence to men have been
> confined prophecy, religious leadership, saintship, pilgrimage rites, the
> giving of evidence in the law-courts, the duties of the holy war, worship in
> the mosque on the day of assembly [Friday], etc. They also have the
> privilege of electing chiefs, have a larger share of inheritance and
> discretion in the matters of divorce.[74]

Here God's preference is interpreted to justify the necessity for the dominance of men

over women. It must be noted, however that such an interpretation conforms to the

---

[73] Al-Ghazali, 89.
[74] Levy, 98-99.

already existing patriarchal culture in which it arose, and which as will be seen informs

the constructed historical narrative written by male historians such as al-Tabari. This

argument for male-domination in Sunni discourse finds similar ground in other religious

literature. As Lerner points out, "Traditionalists….have regarded women's subordination

as universal, God-given or natural, hence immutable Thus it need not be

questioned...The argument may be offered in religious terms: woman is subordinate to

man because she was so created by God."[75]

The third feature that I would like to examine in Sunni gender discourse is the

restriction of women's movement in the public sphere. As Ahmed states, "In Abbasid

society women were conspicuous for their absence from all arenas of the community's

central affairs. In the records relating to this period they are not to be found, as they were

in the previous era, either on the battlefield or in mosques, nor are they described as

participants in or key contributors to the cultural life and productions of their society."[76]

I would like to underline here that the absence of women in the public space, according to

Ahmed, is due more to the indifference of Abbasid historians in recording the everyday

activities of women, not simply because women's movements were more strictly

circumscribed in that space.

Implicit in this discourse, everyday life seems to be divided into two spheres: the

public and the private. In general the private sphere includes the home and activities

taking place within it, while the public sphere comprises activities taking place in the

outside world. There are many analogies one could make between this public/private

---

[75] Lerner, *The Creation of Patriarchy*, 16.
[76] Ahmed, *Women and Gender: Historical Roots of a Modern Debate*, 79.

dichotomy which is a feature of patriarchal cultures in general: "male/female,

honor/shame, outside/inside, active/passive, powerful/powerless, superior/inferior, and

visible/invisible."[77] This patriarchal ideology insists on the restriction of women's

movement and on women exercising independent power outside the domestic sphere,

creating a dependency on men. This exclusionary discourse limiting women's exercise

of social and political power in the Abbasid era was also justified through other *hadiths*

in which the Prophet is supposed to have said, "No people dominated by a woman can

succeed."[78]

This discourse defining the performative roles of women in al-Tabari's time is

primarily informed by the existing patriarchal system in which women were assigned a

subordinate gender role based on their sex. While I am not assuming that this system was

universally applied to women of all classes in the Abbasid era, I am arguing that it was

incorporated in the Sunni discourse during this period. Furthermore, I would like to

argue that such a gender discourse informed al-Tabari's historical narrative and his

representation of women during the Madina period and in the following chapters I will

show how his representation of women in his Madina narrative references such a

discourse.

---

[77] Farha Ghannam, "Public/Private Dichotomy," *Encyclopedia of Women & Islamic Cultures*, ed by Suad
  Joseph, Brill, 2008, Brill Online, American University in Cairo, 23 October 2008 <http://0-
  www.brillonline.nl.lib.aucegypt.edu:80/subscriber/entry?entry=ewic_COM-0139>, par 1.
[78] Al-Ghazali, 98.

Chapter Four

Al-Tabari's Representation of Rebellious Non-Muslim Women

This chapter will attempt to demonstrate that al-Tabari projects his gender assumptions onto his historical narrative of the Madina period, by examining his representation of non-Muslim women during this period. The term non-Muslim here, refers to either pagans or, as will be explained later, women who opposed the Islamic state. Throughout al-Tabari's historical narrative women receive less attention, and when they do appear, he represents them in a manner that affirms his cultural assumptions about gender roles. Although al-Tabari's coverage of the Madina period spans over two thousand pages, covering it in great detail, his narrative demonstrates a logic of inclusion and exclusion; a logic of selection. Historical events and players judged as worthy of mention in his narrative are decided by this logic. Like other male historians of the Abbasid imperial period, al-Tabari focuses his narrative primarily on the achievements of the male elite actors, their military struggles and their state policies. Al-Tabari's narrative betrays such a focus for it is a history, he tells us, of prophets and monarchs and their achievements. One can further argue that his history is primarily one that documents the imperial history of the Arab Muslim state and its achievements.

The first groups of women represented in al-Tabari's history that I would like to examine in this chapter are images of non-Muslim women. In contrast to his ideal representation of Muslim women who seem to fit within his patriarchal/Muslim

assumptions, these non-Muslim women are often constructed as counter examples in

opposition to what he defines as the ideal feminine behavior. These women are usually

shown to exhibit aggressive, domineering, and lewd behavior, for which they are

routinely chastised by other players in al-Tabari's narrative. As 'Umar ibn al-Khattab

commented on one on them, "The vile woman was insolent, and she was habitually base,

since she combined insolence with disbelief." [79]

One could argue that al-Tabari targets these women who belonged to the

opponents of the Muslim Community, representing them in such a way so as to

embarrass or tarnish the image of these opponents. One tactic he often uses is the image

of the female warrior on the non-Muslim side. This is an image that directly contradicts

Abbasid gender norms, which reject women's role in the public activity of war.

However, it was a role that seems to have been accepted by oppositional groups like the

Khawarij during the Umayyad and early Abbasid periods, and from which al-Tabari

establishes a distance. As Leila Ahmed points out:

> With respect to women warriors, the Kharijis argued that, in the case the
> practice was legitimate and indeed a religious requirement for women,
> because women had accompanied Muhammad on his military expeditions
> and fought in his battles. In fact, a number of Khariji women won renown
> for their prowess in battle…The orthodox, who opposed *jihad* for women,
> killed and exposed naked the women captured in their battles with the
> Kharijis—conduct suggesting an attitude toward women on the battlefield
> far different from the first Muslim community. The strategy was effective

---

[79] Tabari, *The History of al-Tabari Volume: VII The Foundation of the Community*, trans by W.
Montgomery Watt and M.V. McDonald (Albany: State University of New York Press, 1987), 130.

in leading Khariji women eventually to withdrawing from the theater of war.[80]

Not only are al-Tabari's accounts silent over the extent of Muslim women participating in battle, it targets the opponents of the Muslim community for accepting such a practice, in an attempt to construct it as an un-Islamic practice that belongs to *jahili* traditions. It is important to observe that al-Tabari's depiction of these aggressive non-Muslim women occur most frequently in those periods when the Muslim Community was in peril, like during the Battle of Uhud or after the death of the Prophet when Abu Bakr faced widespread tribal rebellions. Such a depiction also helps to construct a negative image of the 'other', for it is only the *jahili* opponents of Muslims who allow their women to act, against the accepted gender norms of al-Tabari's culture. One could further argue that al-Tabari may have taken advantage of the vulnerability of these historical moments to target women's behaviors he perceived to be negative.

The Qurashi Women in the Time of the Prophet

The first group of non-Muslim women I would like to examine is the Qurashi women of Mecca. Between the first Islamic year (622CE) and the tenth (632CE) the biggest threat to the Madina Community came from the Qurashi tribe.[81] During this time this Community was in a particularly vulnerable position facing the possibility of extinction. Thus, al-Tabari targets the Qurashi women not only to set up the dynamic of

---

[80] Ahmed, *Women and Gender in Islam: Historical Roots of a Modern Debate*, 53.
[81] Uri Rubin, "Muhammad," *Encyclopaedia of the Qur'an*, ed by Jane Dammen McAuliffe, Georgetown University, Washington DC. Brill, 2009 Brill Online American University in Cairo, 19 February 2009 <http://0-www.brillonline.nl.lib.aucegypt.edu/subscriber/entry?entry=q3_COM-00126>, par 44.

good and bad feminine behavior, but also to idealize the Muslim Community in this period, which he perceived, like other Sunni historians, as a period of great justice.

One way al-Tabari represents Qurashi women and men as the enemy, as the 'other', is his focus on women's role during military battles against the Muslim army of Madina. This is most dramatically seen during the Battle of Uhud (3AH/625CE). While there are some differing accounts of this battle there is agreement that it was a devastating defeat for the Muslims.[82] It was during this vulnerable period that al-Tabari gives attention to depicting the lewdness and domineering behavior of the Qurashi women, and which further demonstrates his view of the dangerous repercussions of women's participation in such public military battles. While in this battle he writes extensively about the Qurashi women's significant role, in other battles where the Muslim army was more successful against Quraysh, such as the Battle of Badr, women are mostly absent or only briefly mentioned in his account.

According to al-Tabari the Qurashi leadership decided to bring along their women to the battle of Uhud in order to prevent the Qurashi men from deserting the battlefield. They believed that if a man did desert the army he would face embarrassment and be mocked by the women, the presence of women therefore was supposed to keep his resolve in fighting. "They had taken their womenfolk with them in the hope that they would be spurred on by zeal to defend these and would not run away."[83] Perhaps in focusing on the presence of Qurashi women al-Tabari is trying to portray the innate

---

[82] C. F. Robinson, "Uhud," *Encyclopaedia of Islam, Second Edition*, ed by P. Bearman et all, Brill, 2009 Brill Online, American University in Cairo, 19 February 2009 <http://0-www.brillonline.nl.lib.aucegypt.edu/subscriber/entry?entry=islam_SIM-7685>, par 3.

[83] Al-Tabari, *The History of al-Tabari Volume: VII The Foundation of the Community*, 107.

weakness in their men, for they had to be pressured to fight in battle. While it seems that it was acceptable for women in the tribal context of the Arabian Peninsula to participate in various ways in the battlefields,[84] it is important to observe how al-Tabari, writing from a different cultural context, emphasized a negative stance vis-à-vis their behavior and presence in this battle.

Once on the battlefield, al-Tabari informs us that the women started to taunt their own men. He gives us a description of the chanting uttered by different Qurashi women throughout the battlefield. "They took up their tambourines. They beat their tambourines behind the men and urged them on to fight." One of them chanted:

> If you advance we will embrace you
> And spread cushions;
> If you turn your backs we will leave you
> And show you no tender love.[85]

It could be argued therefore that the strength of the Qurashi soldiers may have been a result of their fear of losing the love or control of their women. According to al-Tabari's logic of gender, the male soldiers are supposed to be courageous and strong in battle, his narrative of Uhud tends to therefore diminish that male role by emphasizing the aggressive performance of the Qurashi women. Hence their victory was incomplete or was due to their women's aggressive performance.

The women's role in the victory of Uhud is seen in one incident, for example, when al-Tabari reports that the Qurashi men were losing their unity. According to one tribal leader, the strength of an army rests on its banner bearers. "Men are dependent on

---

[84] Abbott, "Women and the State in Early Islam", 263.
[85] Al-Tabari, *The History of al-Tabari Volume: VII The Foundation of the Community*, 118.

what happens to their banners; if their banners are destroyed, they are destroyed too."[86]

Following this passage, we are told that a Muslim soldier killed the man carrying the

Qurashi banner, and it was a woman who picked up and held the banner instead. "The

banner remained flung on the ground until 'Amrah bt. 'Alqamah al-Harithiyyah took hold

of it; she then raised it for Quraysh and they flocked to it."[87] This appears to have rallied

the troops for soon after we are told the Quraysh claimed its victory.

Not only were the Qurashi women shown to be a positive force behind the

efficacy of their men, according to al-Tabari, they seem to have further contributed to the

Qurashi military success by distracting and annoying the Muslim soldiers on the

battlefield. In one instance a Muslim soldier encountered the Qurashi women as they

were chanting against them. He became so annoyed he was about to strike them with his

sword, but refrained from doing so, fearing it would have been disrespectful to the

Prophet:

> He raised his sword to strike them, but then let them be. I said to him, " I
> saw all of your deeds. Why did you decide to lower your sword after
> raising it against the women?" He replied, "I respect the Messenger of
> God's sword too much to kill a woman with it."[88]

This Tabari narrative may also stress the ill-suited nature of women on the battlefield, as

the soldier exercised restraint against killing them. Nevertheless, al-Tabari mentions that

they were frequently targeted for capture, whenever the Muslims' army was in a stronger

military position. "When battle was joined, the polytheists were put to flight, and I saw

---

[86] Al-Tabari, *The History of al-Tabari Volume: VII The Foundation of the Community,* 117.
[87] Ibid, 118-119.
[88] Ibid, 116.

the women tucking up their skirts in flight and exposing their anklets. A cry went up

of "Booty, booty!"[89] Although at first the Muslim troops were discouraged from

following them, later in the battle the idea once again appeared with greater

consequences. "By God, I found myself looking at the anklets of Hind bt. 'Utbah and her

companions as they tucked up their skirts and fled. There was nothing to prevent us

taking them…we had driven the enemy away from [the camp] and thus left our rear

exposed to the cavalry."[90] According to al-Tabari's narrative, the Muslim soldiers

became distracted by the presence of women on the battlefield, and as a result, the

Qurashi soldiers took advantage of such distraction and took control of the field.

Furthermore, the fact that Qurashi women played a vital role in the battlefield

may have been, according to al-Tabari's gender assumptions, a *jahili* practice that should

be rejected by Muslim men. Needless to say, in the more sedentary cultures of Iraq and

Syria, gender roles seem to have been more rigidly defined, and military involvements

were acts generally reserved for men, therefore it is not surprising to see that al-Tabari

perceives the tribal practice of women's participation in battle as an act that diminishes

the masculinity of the men.

While al-Tabari often gives a counter example to the non-Muslim behavior he

finds distasteful, one of the most noticeable aspects of al-Tabari's coverage of these

battles is the lack of Muslim women's presence or any reference given to them. The

exception to this generalization in al-Tabari's history is the Prophet's wife, 'A'isha bint

---

[89] Al-Tabari, *The History of al-Tabari Volume: VII The Foundation of the Community*, 113.
[90] Al-Tabari, *The History of al-Tabari Volume: VII The Foundation of the Community*, 118.

Abi Bakr, during the Battle of the Camel. That case, however, will be dealt with in the next chapter, where it will be analyzed in further depth. Nevertheless, it is important to point out here that when 'A'isha did go onto the battlefield, al-Tabari saw a need to demonstrate counter examples of prominent Muslim women staying at home.[91] Al-Tabari never explicitly tells us that Muslim women were not present during other battles, and in fact, we do have reports from other historical sources telling us that women were present on the Muslim side during these battles.[92] Nevertheless, the fact that he includes no account of their presence demonstrates al-Tabari's gender bias and how he frames the image of the proper Muslim woman who should not be involved in such public military activities.

The battle of Uhud is not the only instance in which al-Tabari uses the image of strong and aggressive Qurashi women to demean the Qurashi male enemy, representing both as belonging to a *jahili,* uncivilized culture. While one could argue that al-Tabari's gender culture idealized the image of the submissive woman, when depicting the Qurashi women, our historian represented them as opposite to that ideal. He even goes to the extent of depicting them as physically abusing Qurashi men. For example, al-Tabari reports, one Qurashi woman after disagreeing with a Qurashi man, "went to one of the tent poles of the enclosure, picked it up and gave him a blow which split his scalp open and made an unpleasant wound…He got up and turned away humiliated."[93] In another instance al-Tabari mentions the case of a strong Qurashi woman who mocked her

---

[91] Al-Tabari, *The History of al-Tabari: Volume XVI The Community Divided,* trans by Adrian Brockett (Albany: State University of New York Press, 1997), 90.

[92] Ahmed, *Women and Gender in Islam: Historical Roots of a Modern Debate,* 53.

[93] Al-Tabari, *The History of al-Tabari Volume: VII The Foundation of the Community,* 69.

husband, questioning his integrity as he was fearfully leaving the house in the middle

of the night. "You are a fighting man; a man of war does not leave his house at an hour

like this."[94]

While these Qurashi women represented in al-Tabari's narrative, serve to

demonstrate the Qurashi male enemy's lack of control and weaknesses, we can also

observe how these actions were often connected to an immoral/uncivilized behavior.

Perhaps the best example of this is al-Tabari's account of the aftermath of the Battle of

Uhud in which he reports how these Qurashi women boasted over their victory, going as

far as committing the crime of mutilating the dead bodies of the Prophet's companions,

al-Tabari reports:

> Hind bint 'Utbah and the women who were with her stopped to mutilate
> the Messenger of God's dead companions, cutting off their ears and noses
> until Hind was able to make anklets and necklaces of them…Then she
> ripped open Hamzah's body for his liver and chewed it, but she was not
> able to swallow it and spat it out. Then she climbed a high rock and
> screamed at the top of her voice the lines of the verse which she had
> spoken when they took possession of the booty they had seized from the
> companions of the Messenger of God.[95]

To express his condemnation of such an act, al-Tabari includes accounts depicting the

abhorrence and shock of the Muslim (civilized) men who watched them. When 'Umar

ibn al-Khattab was asked to describe the incident he stated disapprovingly, "I wish you

had heard what Hind was saying and seen her insolence as she stood on a rock reciting

rajaz-poetry against us and recounting how she had treated Hamzah."[96] Al-Tabari

---

[94] Ibid, 96.
[95] Ibid, 129.
[96] Al-Tabari, *The History of al-Tabari Volume: VII The Foundation of the Community*, 130.

follows this statement with a poem cursing these women for their beliefs and behavior.

Thus our historian connects the uncivilized actions of these women to their disbelief in

Islam.

Following this account, al-Tabari gives a counter representation of a Muslim

woman who performed an opposite, perhaps a more civilized act contrasting to the

Qurashi women's brutality. Here he describes the behavior of a Muslim sister viewing

her brother's remains after they were mutilated.

> The Messenger of God said to her son, al-Zubayr b. al-'Awwam, "Go to
> meet her and turn her back so that she does not see what has happened to
> her brother." Al-Zubayr met her and sad to her, "Mother, the Messenger
> of God commands you to go back." She said, "Why? I have heard that my
> brother has been mutilated, but that is a small thing for the sake of God,
> and I am fully resigned to His will." Al-Zubayr went to the Messenger of
> God and told him this and he said, "Let her come." She came to
> (Hamzah), looked at him, prayed over him, exclaimed, "We belong to God
> and to him do we return, and prayed for his forgiveness."[97]

The inclusion of this passage in his account not only emphasizes the contrasting

difference between the behavior of Qurashi and Muslim women, but it highlights

the uncivilized brutality of the acts of these Qurashi women in mutilating the

bodies of the dead.

Another positive representation of Muslim women, which is implied in al-

Tabari's passage, is their lack of a desire for vengeance. This behavior is consistent with

al-Tabari's image of the docile, but civilized Muslim woman. In contrast, this desire for

vengeance is depicted as a characteristic that he often attributes to non-Muslim Qurashi

---

[97] Ibid, 134.

women. He cites, as another reason explaining why the Qurashi women joined the men on the battlefield of Uhud, is their strong desire for vengeance after their defeat in the first battle of Badr. Many of the Qurashis lost relatives at the Battle of Badr and therefore wanted retaliation. This, he reports, was nowhere truer than among the women. "Every time Hind bt. 'Utbah b. Rabi'ah passed by Wahshi, or he passed by her, she would say, 'Go to it, Abu Dusmah! Quench my thirst for vengeance, and quench your own!'"[98]

In al-Tabari's reports, the Qurashi women appear to be exceptionally brutal in their desire for vengeance. This can be clearly seen in one of his reports of a Qurashi mother.

> When she asked, "My son, who has wounded you?" each replied, "I heard a man saying, when he shot me, 'Take that! I am Ibn al-Aqlah." "The Aqlahi!" she exclaimed, and vowed that if God put her in possession of 'Asim's skull she would drink wine from it.[99]

This report is given a few different versions in al-Tabari's account, but he informs us that such acts of vengeance were against God's will. Once 'Asim did die a Qurashi man wanted to steal his body to sell the skull to the mother, but al-Tabari reports that "God sent a flood in the *wadi* which lifted up 'Asim's body and carried it away."[100]

The Opponents of the Islamic State During the Wars of Apostasy

---

[98] Al-Tabari, *The History of al-Tabari Volume: VII The Foundation of the Community,* 107.
[99] Ibid, 122.
[100] Al-Tabari, *The History of al-Tabari Volume: VII The Foundation of the Community,* 145.

The Prophet died shortly after the defeat of the Quraysh tribe by the army of the Muslims.[101] As the Madina state under Abu Bakr's leadership attempted to consolidate its control of the tribes of Arabia in the wake of the Prophet's death, al-Tabari once again uses women as voices of opposition against the Islamic Community. The death of the Prophet and the ascension of Abu Bakr brought on new turmoil within the Madina state as tribal rebellion spread across the peninsula. While some of the rebelling tribes rejected the religion of Islam, others simply rejected the control of the emerging state in Madina and its new Qurashi leadership. While al-Tabari reports that most of those who rebelled were opposed to Islam, other accounts suggest that many of the tribes merely refused to pay tax, or zakat, to the new state, while not abandoning the faith of Islam.[102] However, to Abu Bakr, the new caliph, there was no distinction between the two, as he is reported to have stated, "I swear by God that I will fight anyone who distinguishes between the salat and zakat."[103] Some of the rebellious women al-Tabari depicts as opponents of Islam may in fact have been following Islamic practices, but only rejecting the controlling authority of the new state, therefore I will include them in the category of non-Muslim women, since this is how they were perceived by al-Tabari.

Generally these tribal rebellions are depicted by Sunni Abbasid historians as Wars of Apostasy. It was a period crucial to the survival of the Madina state, and Islam as a state religion. Abu Bakr's new role as caliph marks a turning point in the development of the state in Madina and later in the surrounding conquered territories. Al-Tabari was a

---

[101] Rubin, par 48.

[102] Alemzadeh, par 66.

[103] Hadi Alemzadeh et all,"Abū Bakr," Encyclopaedia Islamica, ed by Wilferd Madelung and Farhad Daftary, Brill, 2009 Brill Online, American University in Cairo, 18 March 2009
<http://0www.brillonline.nl.lib.aucegypt.edu/subscriber/entry?entry=isla_COM-0046>, par 63.

staunch supporter of Abu Bakr's policies,[104] and therefore he would not want to depict the intricate complexities and nature of these tribal rebellions, for a key component of Sunni Abbasid discourse is the importance of the state's role in appropriating Islam as its raison d'etre. Thus Abu Bakr's move for consolidating state authority over the peninsula is justified by al-Tabari through the more ideological lens of Abu Bakr fighting against apostates to Islam. During this vulnerable period of transition al-Tabari once again targets the women on the opposing side in order to disparage their position. By depicting these women rebels against the state as contrary to the gender discourse of his culture, which al-Tabari assumes to be Islamic, these players may be seen as unbelievers rejecting Islam itself.

One of the more powerful woman rebels, who is depicted by al-Tabari during these Apostasy wars was Salmā bint Rali'ah ibn Fulan. She was the daughter of Umm Qirfah, a powerful tribal woman who in an earlier period opposed the Prophet. Umm Qirfah's power prior to her death was noted by al-Tabari, "The Arabs used to say, 'Had you been more powerful than Umm Qirfah, you could have done no more.'" However, she was killed "cruelly" by a Muslim raiding party lead by Zayd ibn Harithah. "Umm Qirfah suffered a cruel death. He tied her legs with rope and then tied her between two camels until they split her in two. She was a very old woman."[105]

---

[104] C.E. Bosworth, "al-Tabari, Abu Djafar Muhammad b. Djarir b. Yazid", Encyclopaedia of Islam, Second Edition, ed by P. Bearman et all (Brill, 2009 Brill Online. American University in Cairo, 25 February 2009, <http://0-www.brillonline.nl.lib.aucegypt.edu/subscriber/entry?entry=islam_COM-1133>, par 10.

[105] Al-Tabari, *The History of al-Tabari Volume: VIII The Victory of Islam,* trans by Michael Fishbein (Albany: State University of New York Press, 1997), 96.

Then in the following account, al-Tabari informs us that her daughter, Salma, had converted to Islam. Throughout his account al-Tabari seems to implicitly and explicitly connect Salma with 'A'isha, the widow of the Prophet. This connection is first revealed in a report in which Salma is mentioned to be 'A'isha's servant. In this report, A'isha eventually frees Salma and allows her to return to her tribe. Upon the Prophet's death, al-Tabari reports, Salma apostatized from Islam and followed in the rebellious steps of her mother, fighting against the Muslim state.[106] The fact that she followed her mother's footsteps after the death of the Prophet can be seen as a threat to Islamic hegemony, and symbolizes the danger of the Arab tribes reverting back to their tribal autonomy and beliefs. Salma appears to have taken a leadership role in her tribe, contesting the controlling power of the emerging Madina state under Abu Bakr's leadership. Such a position al-Tabari interprets to be a rejection of Islam and therefore it was an act of apostasy. Salma was able to unite the discontented tribal groups to fight with her against the state. "Every company of vanquished warriors and every oppressed person from those clans from Ghatafan and Hawazin and Sulaym and Asad and Tayyi' rallied to her."[107] After gaining a following, al-Tabari reports, Salma then engaged with her warriors in a battle that implicitly resembled 'Aisha's Battle of the Camel, with men fighting and dying around her, while she sat on her camel. Salma, unlike 'A'isha, was not revered as a 'Mother of Believers,' and did not escape death at this battle. "Their

---

[106] Al-Tabari, *The History of al-Tabari Volume: X The Conquest of Arabia,* trans by Fred M. Donner (Albany: State University of New York Press, 1993), 77.
[107] Al- Tabari, *The History of al-Tabari Volume: X The Conquest of Arabia,* 78.

fighting was intense until some horsemen gathered around [Salma's] camel, wounding

it and killing her. Around her camel were slain a hundred men."[108]

Tabari's comparison of Salma to 'A'isha in this event could have many

connotations. It makes 'A'isha's battle not so unique during that period, for it seems that

it was more accepted in tribal culture that elite women could play leading roles in battles.

Adhering to a different gender culture, al-Tabari perceives such participation to be

contrary to women's proper roles, and thus his representation of such battles

demonstrates that the disenfranchised men who followed the leadership of a woman are

bound to meet an ill fate. This coincides with one of the gender traditions attributed to

the Prophet and which circulated widely during the Abbasid era, stating, "No people

dominated by a woman can succeed."[109] Needless to say such gender biases taking on an

Islamic language are strategically used to restrict women's roles in the public sphere. As

will be seen with the other woman leader of these tribal wars, and in the later narrative on

'A'isha's battle, al-Tabari tends to emphasize the power of women to play on the

emotions of men.

According to al-Tabari's account, another woman who fought during the Wars of

Apostasy was Sajah bint Al- Harith. Sajah was a woman who "after the death of the

Apostle of God…pretended to be a prophetess."[110] She was also able to gather groups of

disenfranchised tribes to fight against Abu Bakr. She was temporarily joined by two

other male leaders, who, according to al-Tabari, after realizing "the shamefulness of what

---

[108] Al- Tabari, *The History of al-Tabari Volume: X The Conquest of Arabia*, 79.
[109] Al-Ghazali, 98.
[110] Al- Tabari, *The History of al-Tabari Volume: X The Conquest of Arabia*, 88

they had done" returned home and "behaved humbly".[111] Yet Sajah still fought on and

established an alliance with another "false" prophet who intended to "devour the Arabs

with [his] tribes and [her] tribe" once they were married.[112] As payment of her dowry he

told her, "Call out among your companions that [I], the Apostle of God, has unburdened

you of two of the prayers that Muhammad imposed upon you—the last evening prayer

and the dawn prayer."[113] The purpose of al-Tabari including such negative reports of

Sajah may not only to show the danger and futility of women leading disenfranchised

groups, but also to show the danger of transgressing gender norms. He describes Sajah as

a false prophet, thus accusing her of being an opponent of Islam, who did not behave in

accordance with his "Islamic" gender culture. As her dowry was said to be to change

what the Prophet had already prescribed among Muslims, her representation could be

seen as a warning of the bigger threat of distorting the Prophet's teaching.

Following the accounts of these 'un-Islamic' women, there are no other accounts

focusing on woman leaders in al-Tabari's narrative of the Madina period, until we reach

the account depicting 'A'isha's leading role during the Battle of the Camel. This, despite

the fact that al-Tabari gives us detailed accounts of numerous other battles after these

Wars of Apostasy, during which the Arab tribes conquered the surrounding geographical

regions. The reason for this could be that after the Wars of Apostasy the conquest wars

involved distant territories beyond the Arabian Peninsula and therefore it was less likely

---

[111] Al- Tabari, *The History of al-Tabari Volume: X The Conquest of Arabia*, 98.
[112] Al- Tabari, *The History of al-Tabari Volume: X The Conquest of Arabia*, 95
[113] Al- Tabari, *The History of al-Tabari Volume: X The Conquest of Arabia*, 96.

that women were given leading roles in such wars. This however does not preclude the

possibility that women may have been present during such wars in different capacities.

Chapter Five

Al-Tabari's Representation of 'A'isha's Role in the Battle of the Camel

As shown in the previous chapter, the image of the female warrior is often represented by al-Tabari as one that is un-Islamic, one that belongs to the *jahili* period. Al-Tabari's biased stance on this issue may have been formed not only by his own cultural conditioning, but as Leila Ahmed suggests, as a response to Kharijite oppositional discourse, which for a length of time upheld the significance of women's role in times of war. She points out that the reason for this may have been that "the early Kharijis were Arabs, as distinct from *mawlas*…or Arabs intermingled with *mawlas*…this perhaps was a reason that the Arab tradition of women in battle endured longer among them than among orthodox Muslims, who, following the conquests, became more rapidly assimilated with non-Arabs."[114] Prior to the Battle of the Camel al-Tabari refrains from mentioning Muslim women on the battlefield, despite the fact that there is strong evidence from other sources, like in Ibn Sa'd and Baladhuri, of their presence.[115] While it is true the Muslim women which other medieval scholars denote during these battles did not participate in combat, the fact that al-Tabari omits even mentioning Muslim women in connection to the battlefield, up until 'A'isha, could be seen as significant. Nevertheless, because of the importance of the Battle of the Camel and 'A'isha bint Abi

---

[114] Ahmed, *Women and Gender in Islam: Historical Roots of a Modern Debate*, 71-72.

[115] Ahmed, *Women and Gender in Islam: Historical Roots of a Modern Debate*, 69-72: and Nabia Abbott, "Women and the State on the Eve of Islam," *American Journal of Semitic Languages and Literature 58, no. 3 (Jul., 1941): 277.*

Bakr's vital role in it, al-Tabari could not disregard the event, despite the fact that her military role runs contrary to Abbasid cultural traditions regarding such military practices.

Therefore, rather than ignoring 'A'isha's role in the Battle of the Camel one finds that al-Tabari's account focuses on it, by representing the battle as an issue over female public participation in military confrontations, rather than an issue over 'Uthmān ibn 'Affān's assassination. The focus in al-Tabari's account of this battle is almost entirely pre-occupied with whether 'A'isha should have been permitted to leave the house. According to al-Tabari, she was acting not only contrary to Qur'anic injunctions, but also contrary to the perceived Abbasid gender ideals. Thus our historian's concern was not so much who held the right position in this battle, 'Ali or his three opponents who formed the opposition, but for al-Tabari it was more about whether it was appropriate for 'Aisha as a woman to participate in a public activity that in his culture was traditionally reserved for men only.

Al-Tabari's Account of 'A'isha's Motive for Opposing 'Ali's Caliphate

'A'isha is the only Muslim woman al-Tabari mentions to have had a political leading role during the Madina period. Her motive for taking up this role, however, remains elusive in al-Tabari's account. While many times in his narrative 'A'isha is made to state that her reason for opposing the new caliph 'Ali was to seek just retribution for the death of 'Uthman, nonetheless al-Tabari often alludes to her dislike of 'Ali as the primary motive for her opposition. He reports that once 'A'isha was informed of 'Ali's ascension to the caliphate, she became immediately distressed, believing it was a mob

mentality that allowed him to rule in Madina. This prompted her to spring into political

action:

> "What news?" she asked. He kept silent and then muttered something.
> Confound you! Is it bad for us or good?" "You don't know! 'Uthman
> was killed, and they wait eight nights." "Then what do they do?" she
> asked. "They made the men of Medina agree to elect 'Ali, and the city is
> under the control of the rebels." At this she returned to Mecca and said
> not a word. Indeed she said nothing until she had dismounted at the door
> of the mosque, gone to the Hijr, and curtained herself off, and the people
> had gathered round.
>
> "People of Mecca!" She said. "The mob of men from the garrison cities
> and the watering places and the slaves of the people of Medina have
> conspired together. They charged this man who was killed yesterday with
> deceit, with putting young men in high positions where older ones had
> been before, and with reserving certain specially protected places for
> them, although they had been arranged before him and could not properly
> be charged. Nevertheless he went along with these people, and in an
> attempt to pacify them he withdrew from these policies. When they could
> then find neither real argument nor excuse, they became irrational. They
> showed their hostility openly, and their deeds didn't fit their words. They
> spilled forbidden blood, they violated the sacred city, they appropriated
> sacred money, and they profaned the sacred month. By Allah! One of
> Uthman's fingers is better than a whole world of their type. Save
> yourselves from being associated with them, and let others punish them
> and their followers be scared off. By Allah! Even if what they recon
> against him were a crime he would have been cleaned of it, as gold is
> cleaned of its impurities or a garment of its dirt, for they have rinsed him
> as a garment is rinsed with water."[116]

Following this address, al-Tabari reports that the crowd was screaming for revenge. This

clearly demonstrates al-Tabari's belief in 'A'isha's effectiveness at stirring up the

emotions of the Meccan audience, by creating an image of a community hurdling towards

disarray as its honorable leader, who attempted in vain to appease the mob, was unjustly

---

[116] Al-Tabari, *The History of al-Tabari: Volume XVI The Community Divided*, 38-39.

murdered. While in this address, she never specifically accuses 'Ali of any misdeed, she attacks the current power structure for not pursuing justice, portraying it as weak.

Yet al-Tabari seems skeptical in 'A'isha's expressed desire for justice, showing how she held earlier mixed feelings regarding 'Uthman's leadership. In one passage, al-Tabari points out that it was 'Ali, not 'A'isha who was willing to assist 'Uthman during his time of need:

> ['Uthman] dispatched one of 'Amr's sons to 'Ali [with the message]: "They have denied us water. If you can send us some do so." [He sent the same message] to Talha and al-Zubayr, and to 'A'ishah and the other wives of the Prophet. The first to come to his aid were 'Ali and Umm Habibah. 'Ali came shortly before dawn and said, "O people, neither believers nor unbelievers act like this. Do not cut off supplies from this man. The Romans and Persians give food and drink to their captives. This man did not resist you, so how can you think it lawful to besiege and kill him?" "No, by God, we will show no mercy," they answered. "We will not let him eat or drink." Then ('Ali) threw down his turban in the house [and said], "I have done what you asked me to do." He went home…
>
> 'A'isha was filled with rancor against the Egyptians. Marwan b. al-Hakam came to her and said, "Mother of the Faithful, if you remained [in Medina] they would be more likely to show respect to this man." She responded, "Do you want me to be treated as Umm Habibah was?[117] I find no one who will defend me. No, by God, I am not to be blamed. I do not know what the actions of these people will lead to."[118]

Further, not only does al-Tabari tell us that 'A'isha would not assist 'Uthman in that critical period, he informs that she tried to generate dissent among others over his rule, with the hope that Talhah would eventually acquire the caliphate. This is shown in a report where she confronts one of the caliph's influential supporters, Ibn 'Abbās:

---

[117] Al-Tabari reports Umm Habibah being driven out of town by the crowd besieging 'Uthman's house.

[118] Al-Tabari, *The History of al-Tabari: Volume XV The Crisis of the Early Caliphate*, trans by Stephen R. Humphreys (Albany: State University of New York Press, 1990), 208-209.

> She said, "Ibn 'Abbas, I entreat you by God: abandon ['Uthman], sow doubt
> about him among the people, for you have been given a sharp tongue.
> Their powers of discernment have been clarified, the beacon light is raised
> high to guide them, and (the Caliphs's associates) have milked the lands
> that once abounded in good things. I have seen Talhah b. 'Ubaydallah
> take possession of the keys to the public treasuries and storehouses. If he
> became caliph, he will follow in the path of his paternal cousin Abu
> Bakr."
>
> According to (Ibn 'Abbas): I said, "O Mother (of the Believers), if some
> evil were to befall that man [namely, 'Uthman], the people would seek
> asylum only with our companion [namely, 'Ali]." She replied, "Be quiet!
> I have no desire to defy or quarrel with you."[119]

In his accounts Al-Tabari continues to build doubt over 'Aisha's motives by including

many conversations in his narrative of people strongly questioning them in fighting

against 'Ali. This is clearly seen in one conversation that 'A'isha is reported to have held

with Ibn Umm Kilab:

> "By Allah! 'Uthman has been killed unjustly, I will seek revenge for his
> blood!" Ibn Umm Kilab said to her: "How is that? By Allah! You were
> the first to incline the blade against 'Uthman and were saying 'Kill Na'thal
> [literally: hyena, referring to 'Uthman], for he has become a
> disbeliever!'"[120]

In his efforts to dilute 'A'isha's motive to seek justice for the death of 'Uthman, al-Tabari

is able to change the event's focal point to another issue: whether 'A'isha should have

been permitted to take a role in the battle. This point is stressed in another report, where

after 'A'isha gives a public speech on the need to seek justice for 'Uthman's death, in the

town of al-Mirbad, the crowd divides into two groups: one group supporting her and one

group opposing her. Of those who opposed her one man is supposed to have told her:

---

[119] Al-Tabari, *The History of al-Tabari: Volume XV The Crisis of the Early Caliphate*, 238-9.
[120] Al-Tabari, *The History of al-Tabari: Volume XVI The Community Divided*, 53.

> Mother of the Faithful! By Allah! The killing of 'Uthman b. 'Affan is a lesser
> matter than your coming out from your house on this accursed camel,
> exposing yourself to armed combat! Allah curtained you off and gave you
> sanctity. You have torn down the curtain and profaned your sanctity.
> Anyone who thinks you should be fought also thinks you should be killed.
> If you have come to us obedient, then return home![121]

Al-Tabari's Focus on 'A'isha's Responsibility to Stay at Home

Al-Tabari includes many accounts of the utter brutalities committed during the

Day of the Camel. This was the first major battle, from the Sunni perspective, between

two groups of committed Muslims. While it could be argued that the Ridda War was the

first civil war in the Muslim community, this was the first battle in which high profile

Companions of the Prophet fought each other. According to one eyewitness, "On the

Day of the Camel we shot arrows at each other until there were no more to shoot, and we

stabbed each other with spears until they were enmeshed in our chests and theirs. Had

horses been made to walk over them they could have."[122]

D.A. Spellberg comments that the following generations of historians, in both the

Shi'i and Sunni sources, generally place blame on 'A'isha's public action for the carnage

which took place during the battle. Furthermore these medieval historians used her

action as proof of the disastrous outcome of women's participation in politics. "Her

example would be cited by Sunni and Shi'i Muslims alike when the issue of female

involvement in government arose. Her depiction, most particularly with reference to the

first civil war in the Muslim community, reflected the crystallization of Islamic

---

[121] Al-Tabari, *The History of al-Tabari: Volume XVI The Community Divided*, 61.
[122] Al-Tabari, *The History of al-Tabari: Volume XVI The Community Divided*, 156.

definitions of gender and politics."[123] The notoriety of 'A'isha's place as the leader of

the battle was marked by the name of the battle itself. It denotes where 'A'isha sat during

the fighting as she guided the military forces around her. In fact, her troops were even

named by their opponents "the Companions of the Camel" because the heaviest fighting

is reported to have taken place at 'A'isha 's feet.[124]   Al-Tabari adherence to this view can

be seen in one passage in which the three leaders decide to go to Basra to gain support:

> [Talha and al-Zubayr's] minds had been made up to go to al-Basrah they
> said, "Mother of the Faithful, leave Medina alone! Those with us aren't
> sufficient for that mob there. Accompany us to al-Basrah. We will arrive
> at a city lost to us. They will produce their allegiance to 'Ali b. Abi Talib
> as an argument against us, but you will mobilize them, just as you did with
> the Meccans. Then you will be able to sit back, and, if Allah puts things
> right, it will be as you want. If not, we will leave things to Him and do
> our best to push the case forward until Allah executes His will."
> "Agreed!" she said on hearing this—for the matter could be resolved only
> by her.[125]

'A'isha's role in the battle produces a major conflict for al-Tabari. According to him, not

only was it a public rejection of Abbasid gender norms, she is directly disobeying God's

command which is stated in the Qur'an:

> O wives of the Prophet! You are not like any other of the women; If you
> will be on your guard, then be not soft in (your) speech, lest he in whose
> heart is a disease yearn; and speak a good word. And stay in your houses
> and do not display your finery like the displaying of the ignorance of yore;
> and keep up prayer, and pay the poor-rate, and obey Allah and His
> Messenger. Allah only desires to keep away the uncleanness from you, O
> people of the House! And to purify you a (thorough) purifying.[126]

---

[123] Spellberg, 101.
[124] Spellberg, 106.
[125] Al-Tabari, *The History of al-Tabari: Volume XVI The Community Divided*, 41.
[126] Verse 33:32-33.

While this command was directed towards her and the Prophet's other wives, by the Abbasid period it appears to have been extended as a prescribed norm to other Muslim women.[127] Therefore the fact that 'Aisha out of all women disregarded it must be given attention in Sunni historical accounts. For while Shi'i scholarship had the luxury to distance itself from 'A'isha, within Sunni scholarship she plays the role of politically linking the first caliph Abu Bakr and Muhammad.[128] 'A'isha's thus serves not only as a reflection of the honor of the Prophet, but the honor of the first caliph and his right to have taken the leadership of the Islamic Community after the death of the Prophet.

Therefore, as D.A. Spellberg argues, "Sunni historiography sought to invalidate 'A'isha's participation without making her completely responsible for the carnage of the first civil war."[129] Because within the Sunni tradition 'A'isha is noted to be Muhammad's favorite wife, it is difficult to represent her as acting in a less than ideal manner. Al-Tabari adheres to such a stance, demonstrating 'A'isha's special status by noting how the caliph 'Umar ibn al-Khattab gave preference to her because of Muhammad's special relationship with her. Al-Tabari tells us, "He gave 'A'ishah two thousand dirhams more than to the others because the Prophet loved her, but she did not accept that."[130] In addition, 'A'isha is recorded in his account as saying, "I was one of the dearest people to him; a verse of the Qur'an was revealed concerning me when the community was almost destroyed;[131] I saw Gabriel when none of his other wives saw

---

[127] Ahmed, *Women and Gender in Islam: Historical Roots of a Modern Debate*, 68.

[128] Spellberg, 4.

[129] Spellberg, 108.

[130] Al-Tabari, *The History of al-Tabari: Volume XII The Battle of al-Qadishiyyah and the Conquest of Syria and Palestine*, 202.

[131] Referencing the "Account of Adultery" resulting in the Qur'anic verse 24:11.

him; and he was taken (that is, dead) in his house when there was nobody with him but the angel and myself."[132]

Controversy over 'A'isha 's behavior, in al-Tabari's account, is also reported through the comments of many persons, both named and unnamed. Most notable of these was one of Muhammad's other wives Umm Salamah. In al-Tabari's narrative Umm Salamah plays the useful role of being an advocate for Abbasid gender norms. While she disagreed with 'A'isha's motive for opposing 'Ali, she also disagreed with 'A'isha's leaving the house. Therefore, instead of criticizing 'A'isha directly al-Tabari expresses his criticism through Umm Salamah. While the latter stayed at home during the battle, she sent her son in her place. Umm Salamah is reported to have said to 'Ali as he was leaving for the battle, "Commander of the Faithful! But for the fact that I would be disobeying Allah and that you wouldn't accept it from me, I would come out with you. But here is my son 'Umar—dearer to me than my very self, by Allah! He will come out with you and will be there with you at your battles."[133] As will be shown in chapter six, Umm Salmah also plays another unique role in Tabari's account, for she appears to be the only wife, apart from Khadija, to have advised the Prophet during his lifetime. Spellberg agrees that Umm Salamah is often used in Sunni scholarship to combat the legacy of 'A'isha, for although 'A'isha, within Sunni scholarship, is often acknowledged as the 'favorite' wife of the Prophet, she argues that Umm Salamah can be seen to be the 'wisest'.[134]

---

[132] Al-Tabari, *The History of al-Tabari: Volume VII The Foundation of the Community*, 7.
[133] Al-Tabari, *The History of al-Tabari: Volume XVI The Community Divided*, 42.
[134] Spellberg, 137.

In addition to Umm Salamah, al-Tabari tells us that 'A'isha's act was denounced by other Muslims who were previously loyal to her, because, as he suggests, she ignored the Qur'anic command to stay at home:

> When 'A'ishah arrived at al-Basrah, she wrote to Zayd b. Suhan: "From 'A'ishah bint Abi Bakr, Mother of the Faithful, beloved of the Messenger of God, to her devoted son Zayd b. Suhan. After greetings. When this letter of mine reaches you, come and assist us in this undertaking! If you don't, then at least make the people abandon 'Ali." He wrote back to her: "From Zayd b. Suhan to 'A'ishah bint Abi Bakr al-Siddiq, beloved of the Messenger of God. After greeting. If you withdraw from this undertaking and return home, then I will be your devoted son. If you don't, I will be the first to break with you." "May Allah have mercy on the Mother of the Faithful!" said Zayd b. Suhan. "She was ordered to stay at home, and we were ordered to fight. But she didn't do what she was ordered and ordered us to do it, and she did what we were ordered and ordered us not to do it!"[135]

Whether or not 'A'isha had right cause to oppose 'Ali was not the issue for many, al-Tabari reports, rather it was the fact that she acted like the women from the jahiliyya period, which for him was unacceptable for a Muslim woman. Women's political participation in the public sphere was an act that al-Tabari wished to link to women of the *jahiliyya,* or other non-believers. Thus, in many passages, al-Tabari tries to illustrate the damage that 'A'isha's involvement caused, displaying its destructive effects, showing this to be an unwise act for a Muslim woman. For instance, he demonstrates that her place on the battlefield had caused unnecessarily increased bloodshed. "When the others gathered round 'A'ishah, and the Kufans were insisting on fighting, with 'A'ishah as their only target, she urged on her own men, and they fought on."[136] In another passage

---

[135] Al-Tabari, *The History of al-Tabari: Volume XVI The Community Divided,* 79-80.
[136] Al-Tabari, *The History of al-Tabari: Volume XVI The Community Divided,* 133.

he records, "Seventy men were killed that day, each holding in turn the nose rein of

'A'ishah's camel."[137]

After the battle was over, al-Tabari further highlights 'A'isha's involvement by

including poems of lament by some of the soldiers who opposed her. In them they

clearly blame her for rejecting her gender role of being the mother of believers:

> O Mother of ours! The most refractory mother we know!
> A mother [normally] feeds a son and shows him mercy.
> Have you not seen how many a brave is being wounded,
> his hand and wrist made lonely?[138]

While in al-Tabari's account 'A'isha never directly expresses regret for her action, she

can be seen to have expresses remorse on two occasions for the outcome of her actions:

> "Who are you?" she asked. "An Azdi tribesman living in Kufah." "Were
> you present with us on the Day of the Camel?" "Yes." "For us or against
> us?" "Against," I replied. "Do you know then who it was who said:
> 'Mother of ours! O best Mother we know?" "I do," I replied. "It was my
> paternal cousin," and she wept so bitterly I thought she was not going to
> stop.[139]

In another passage after one man informs her of the dead incurred as a result of the battle

she is reported to have said, "By Allah! Had I but died two decades before this day!"[140]

Although al-Tabari's account seems to suggest that the reason for the bloodshed is

because 'A'isha disobeyed God's commands, his reports include less expressed regret

than in other medieval narratives of the event. For example, Ibn Sa'd reports that 'A'isha

wished to be "completely forgotten" because of her actions. Further he records that prior

---

[137] Ibid, 127.
[138] Ibid, 137.
[139] Ibid, 141-142.
[140] Ibid, 162.

to her death she decided that she did not deserve to be buried with the Prophet, as she

had planed to do previously. "I caused wrongdoing after the Prophet. So they should

bury me with the [other] wives of the Prophet."[141] It could be argued that the reason al-

Tabari records less of 'A'isha's feelings of guilt is in order to stress the blame on the

weakness of her gender, not herself. It was female nature, not 'A'isha, he could be telling

us, to put our blame on.

While 'A'isha's actions along with her duplicitous motives may be seen to reflect

poorly upon the 'Mother of the Faithful', al-Tabari avoids direct negative depictions of

her, instead he attacks the female nature and its ill fit to politics. As Spellberg observes

in her study of Sunni accounts, "'A'isha is the object of both praise and blame, praise as

the wife of the Prophet and blame for her political actions as his widow…Ultimately,

'A'isha's political legacy was transformed into a convenient component of the medieval

cultural construct which defined all women as threats to the maintenance of Islamic

political order."[142]

This attitude is reflected in al-Tabari's account, where 'Ali is shown to have

placed little blame on 'A'isha. Soon after the fighting ended, he is reported to have made

amends with 'A'isha:

> 'A'isha commenting, "By Allah! There was never anything in the past
> between me and 'Ali other than what usually happens between a woman
> and her male in-laws. In my opinion he has shown himself one of the best
> of men, despite my criticism." 'Ali in turn affirmed 'A'isha's continual
> place as the wife of the Prophet, "She has spoken the truth and nothing but

---

[141] Spellberg, 119.
[142] Ibid, 109.

the truth. That was all there was between us. She's the wife of your Prophet now and forever."[143]

'Ali's forgiveness may be explained in gender terms, especially in an earlier speech where he instructs his men not to treat women like themselves, for "they are weak". [144]

The Responsibility of the Two Companions for the Battle in Al-Tabari's Account

One solider in al-Tabari's account warns, "O 'Aysha! The people around you are actually enemies."[145] If according to al-Tabari's account, direct criticism is not expressed against 'A'isha for her participation, perhaps one must look to the two other male Companions who seem to be directly blamed for 'Aisha's actions. In patriarchal discourse there is a strong assumption that the actions of the female members of a family reflect upon its male members and on their ability to control or protect them.[146] Al-Tabari's culture is reflected in his reporting, for while he does place some shame on 'A'isha for her actions, I would like to argue that he attributes her faulty behavior to her weak female nature. In this way it appears as though more dishonor is to be placed on the two male Companions whose responsibility it was to stop her from going public. Instead, al-Tabari reports, they not only permitted such an action but went so far as to encourage it as well.

---

[143] Al-Tabari, *The History of al-Tabari: Volume XVI The Community Divided,* 170.
[144] Ibid, 165.
[145] Ibid, 134.
[146] Lerner, *The Creation of Patriarchy,* 80.

In al-Tabari's account, the two companion's motive, like 'A'isha, is put into question by those around them.[147] Although they, like 'A'isha, state that they were fighting the caliph in order to uphold justice for 'Uthman's murder, al-Tabari notes that both of them similarly rejected helping 'Uthman when he was being refused water and food by the Egyptians. "When Talhah and al-Zubayr heard what had happened to 'Ali and Umm Habibah, they stayed in their homes."[148] In some of al-Tabari's reports there is insinuation that their motive was based on their desire for power and the caliphate. In one passage a companion of the two notes, "If victory had been ours we would have been caught up in civil war: Al-Zubayr wouldn't have let Talha rule, nor would Talha have let al-Zubayr."[149] However, it is interesting to observe that while they are occasionally berated for opposing the new caliph, they are criticized more harshly by other actors in al-Tabari's account for their support of 'A'isha's public role.

After the death of the Prophet, it could be argued that his wives stood in contradiction to the Abbasid gender view of how 'proper' women should behave. As Ahmed contends, "All were independent women—specifically, women who were not living under the authority of any man—a condition that orthodox Islam was to require for women…It is somewhat ironic that such a configuration should mark the early history of a religion that, in the orthodox view, frowns on celibacy and requires women always to live under the authority of men."[150] Similarly, it could be argued that al-Tabari tries to mitigate the independence of these women by placing the responsibility for their actions

---

[147] Al-Tabari, *The History of al-Tabari: Volume XVI The Community Divided*, 97.

[148] Al-Tabari, *The History of al-Tabari: Volume XV The Crisis of the Early Caliphate*, 208-209.

[149] Al-Tabari, *The History of al-Tabari: Volume XVI The Community Divided*, 46-47.

[150] Ahmed, *Women and Gender in Islam: Historical Roots of a Modern Debate*, 74.

upon the male Community of Muslims, and mainly upon those men who permitted

them to act outside of the 'accepted' norms.

Many times in al-Tabari's account the two Companions are condemned for their

hypocrisy in allowing the wife of the Prophet to do what they would not permit their own

wives to do. As one group of people reported to 'Ali, "They then came to their mother,

the wife of the Messenger of Allah, and they approved for her what they disapproved of

for their own wives and exposed her to things that were taboo to them and were no

good."[151] A young slave boy also is reported to have reprimanded both of the

Companions when they asked the tribe of the Banu Sa'd to join them:

> "As for you, Zubayr, you are the disciple of the Messenger of Allah, and
> as for you Talha, you preserved the Messenger of Allah with your own
> hand. I see your Mother is with you. Have you brought your wives too?"
> "No," they both replied. "I have nothing to do with you then," the Sa'dī
> said and withdrew. He said the following verses about this:
>
> You preserved the honor of your wives yet led out your mother.
> By Allah! There is little justice in this!
> She was commanded to trail her hems at home, but she had a whim to
> cross the deserts at the gallop.
> [Making herself] a target that her sons must defend by fighting with
> arrows and Khattī spears and swords.
> Her curtains have been ripped down by Talha and al-Zubayr.
> No further tale needs to be told about them![152]

While 'A'isha was perhaps the Prophet's most powerful wife, Ahmed reports that she

was closely followed by another one of his wives:

> 'Aisha and Hafsa, as daughters of the first two caliphs, Abu Bakr and
> 'Umar, enjoyed even further prestige and influence. Both Abu Bakr and
> 'Umar, just prior to their deaths, entrusted their daughters, rather than their

---

[151] Al-Tabari, *The History of al-Tabari: Volume XVI The Community Divided*, 101.
[152] Ibid, 62.

sons, with important responsibilities. During his last illness Abu Bakr made 'Aisha responsible for disposing of certain public funds and properties and distributing his own property among his other grown sons and daughters. At 'Umar's death the first copy of the Quran, which had been in Abu Bakr's possession and then in 'Umar's, passed into Hafsa's keeping.[153]

Notable in al-Tabari's account, Hafsa is reported to have agreed with 'A'isha and wanted to join her in leading the battle, however she was stopped from doing so by a male family member:

> Hafsah wanted to go with them, but 'Abdallah b. 'Umar came and asked her to stay. She stayed but sent a message to 'A'ishah: "Abdallah has prevented me from coming out." "May Allah forgive him!" said 'A'isha.[154]

This could be interpreted as a further display of the responsibility of strong men in restricting women's involvement in the public military sphere. If the two Companions restricted 'A'isha like 'Abdallah did to Hafsah, it could be argued that the bloodshed would not have occurred. Ultimately the two Companions paid a higher price for their role in the event than 'A'isha. After fleeing the battle Al-Zubayr was stabbed from behind while preparing to pray,[155] and al-Tabari reports to us that Talhah died in shame, after being hit with an arrow by an unknown archer. As he slowly died he requested, from his slave, "Find me a place where no one knows me. I've never seen an old man lose so much blood as today."[156]

---

[153] Ahmed, *Women and Gender in Islam: Historical Roots of a Modern Debate*, 74.
[154] Al-Tabari, *The History of al-Tabari: Volume XVI The Community Divided*, 41-42.
[155] Al-Tabari, *The History of al-Tabari: Volume XVI The Community Divided*, 159.
[156] Al-Tabari, *The History of al-Tabari: Volume XVI The Community Divided*, 150.

Chapter Six

Al-Tabari's Representation of the Muslim Woman Advisor

Genevieve Lloyd argues, "Ideas of maleness have developed under the guise of supposedly neutral ideals of Reason."[157] Such 'neutral ideals of Reason' said to be characteristic of hegemonic masculinity in some Western discourses may be said to also characterize hegemonic masculine culture during the Abbasid period. While the feminine is assigned the attribute of emotionality in this discourse, the male is assigned the attribute of reason. This is demonstrated in the aforementioned *tafsir* in which al-Ghazali remarks, "Allah has preferred the one sex over the other in the matter of mental ability and good counsel, and in their power for the performance of duties and for carrying out of [divine] commands."[158] Lloyd further explains how the assigning of reason to maleness helps ensure female suppression:

> Hegel's diagnosis of "womankind,"…occurs in a wider framework, which endorses the relegation of women to the private domain. But his understanding of the complexity, and the pathos, of gender difference in some ways transcends that. He saw that life in the nether world has conditioned the modes of female consciousness; that the distinctively "feminine" is not a brute face, but a structure largely constituted through suppression.[159]

Once such an ideological framework is appropriated in a cultural context, the emotional

---

157 Genevieve Lloyd, "From the Man of Reason," in *Gender,* ed by Carol C. Gould (New Jersey: Humanities Press, 1997), 228.
158 Levy, 98-99.
159 Lloyd, 227.

as a feminine attribute may be seen to be less destructive in the private sphere, while

reason as an attribute of the male is proven to be most beneficial as the dominant factor in

both the public and private sphere. I am trying to show here that one important lesson

that al-Tabari tries to push forward in his accounts of women's participation in military

battles, is the idea that women cannot be effective leaders because of their emotional

tendencies. While they may be productive in rallying troops, because of their emotional

appeal, our historian represents them as being unable to use this power rationally, and as

we have seen in his historical accounts of battles where women held some leading

positions, the account ends in insinuating that the disastrous outcome may have happened

because of such participation. This masculinist stance on the part of al-Tabari coincides

with the popular hadith attributed to the Prophet in which he is supposed to have said,

"No people dominated by a woman can succeed."[160]

Even though al-Tabari's historical narrative is replete with instances

demonstrating the emotionality of women, depicting them as jealous, fragile, and erratic,

there are some instances in which he represents women as rational and wise, thus

contradicting the masculinist discourse that perceives women as irrational and therefore

incapable of taking reasonable decision making. In this chapter I would like to explore

al-Tabari's representation of women as rational figures who take on the role of advisors

to male family members. However, I would like to argue that even though al-Tabari's

accounts give strong evidence that these women possessed good judgment of character,

his accounts seems to serve and highlight his masculine cultural norms, in such a manner

---

[160] Al-Ghazali, 98.

that supports the prescription of women's use of their rational power. In his narrative women advisors appear not only in relation to the Prophet, but also in relation to the succeeding Madina caliphs. While such cases may illustrate the value of women as advisors in matters of the public sphere, the representation of such cases retain women in a secondary position, for they are meant only to be of service to their male family members, they are not the ultimate decisions-makers. Such decision-making is ultimately assigned to men in positions of authority and power. Furthermore, these women prove to be the exceptions not the rule, and, as will be demonstrated, their representation as advisors affirms the orthodox or hegemonic gender norms of the Abbasid period. As al-Tabari insinuates it is only those women who subscribed to this relationship of power in which men are in authority over women, whose rational decisions may lead to beneficial results for the Muslim Community or the family.

One of the first points to note about al-Tabari's representation of female advisors is how their manner is depicted as vastly different from the other women who were involved in the public sphere. Thus, unlike the Qurashi women or the other women opponents to the Muslim community, the women advisors that are depicted in positive terms in al-Tabari's accounts are assigned positive attributes: they are good Muslims, docile and obedient to male authority. In contrast to the Qurashi and other rebellious women who appropriate leadership roles, these women are identified as playing the proper role that a Muslim woman should play, acting as advisors to those men in authority.

One early figure that seems to exemplify the gender ideals of the Abbasid period is the Prophet's wife Umm Salamah. While the Prophet has a noted history of seeking the counsel of his first wife Khadija,[161] during the Madina period Umm Salamah is the only wife in al-Tabari's accounts who appears to play the role of advisor to the Prophet. One example of the Prophet taking into account the wisdom of Umm Salamah occurs after he was upset by the behavior of some of his followers. According to one of al-Tabari's accounts, the Prophet's followers refrained from following his orders when he asked them, "Arise, sacrifice, and shave."[162] Noting their reluctance, Umm Salamah wisely advised him the following, "Go out, and speak not a word to any of them until you have slaughtered your fattened camel and summoned your shaver to shave you." After abiding by this advice, to lead by example, the Prophet's followers were quick to obey him and all felt a surge of guilt for not doing so before.[163] While this passage displays the wisdom of Umm Salamah and her ability to advice the Prophet in this situation, it also demonstrates how the Prophet by following her advise showed confidence in her judgment.

Al-Tabari's representation of Umm Salamah playing the role of advisor to her husband demonstrates how she played her role in the 'proper' fashion for a woman, acting only as an advisor through her husband who is then the authority to put that advice into action. Such a representation contrasts with al-Tabari's negative representation of

---

[161] Barbara Freyer Stowasser, "Khadija," *Encyclopaedia of the Qur'an*, ed by Jane Dammen McAuliffe, Georgetown University, Washington DC. Brill, 2009, Brill Online, The American University in Cairo, 02 April 2009 <http://0-www.brillonline.nl.lib.aucegypt.edu/subscriber/entry?entry=q3_SIM-00247>, par 2.

[162] Al- Tabari, *The History of al-Tabari Volume: VIII The Victory of Islam*, 88.

[163] Al- Tabari, *The History of al-Tabari Volume: VIII The Victory of Islam*, 89.

'Aisha taking on the active leadership of a military operation, whose public role in such an event must have been regarded as reminiscent of *'jahili'* behavior by our Abbasid historian. However, the fact that the more emotional 'A'isha is stated to be the Prophet's preferred wife could insinuate that rationality is not seen as the most important attribute of the favored wife.

After the death of the Prophet, al-Tabari demonstrates that the tradition of women acting as advisors continued with the caliphs of Madina.   At a critical point in his caliphate, the third caliph, 'Uthman ibn 'Affan, questioned whether to follow one of his close advisors, Marwan, or to ally himself with 'Ali ibn Abi Talib. He asked his wife which course was the wisest and she responded:

> You should fear God alone, who has no partner, and you should adhere to the practice of your two predecessors [namely, Abu Bakr and 'Umar]. For if you obey Marwan he will inspire neither awe nor love. The people have only abandoned you due to Marwan's place [in your councils]. Send 'Ali, then, and trust in his honesty and uprightness. He is related to you, and he is not a man who people disobey.[164]

'Uthman agreed with her and followed her advice. However it was to no avail, for 'Ali already swore not to return to Medina to assist the caliph. Once Marwan discovered the advice given against him he angrily went to 'Uthman and complained about the caliph giving preference to his wife's words. 'Uthman retorted, "You are not to say a thing about her! How evil is your countenance! By God, she is a better advisor to me than you are."[165] While these seem to be powerful words in defense of the wife's capacity for wise

---

[164] Al- Tabari, *The History of al-Tabari: Volume XV The Crisis of the Early Caliphate*, trans by Stephen R. Humphreys, (Albany: State University of New York Press, 1990), 178.
[165] Al- Tabari, *The History of al-Tabari: Volume XV The Crisis of the Early Caliphate*, 179.

advice, 'Uthman ultimately accepts Marwan's counsel, which in turn leads to a growth in his unpopularity and eventually creates a split in the Muslim Community.[166]

Based on al-Tabari's account, it appears that the fault lied not with his wife's advice, but in 'Uthman's lack of persistence in pursuing it. For if he continued, after this initial rejection of 'Ali, to try to ally with him and if he had shunned his other advisor Marwan, perhaps 'Uthman's caliphate could have had a less disastrous ending. Although 'Uthman's wife is represented in al-Tabari's account to have made the better decision, al-Tabari does not report that she was angered by his rejection of it. Rather, al-Tabari tells us that she nonetheless continued to support her husband. Such a representation, one could argue, falls within the image of the dutiful wife, so idealized in the gender discourse of the Abbasid era. Al- Tabari tells us that even when 'Uthman was under threat of being murdered, his wife continued to shield him, losing four of her fingers in the attack—a role she was praised for in many of al-Tabari's reports. [167] In fact the role of 'Uthman's wife in the attack was used as an excuse by Mu'awiya (the founder of the Umayyad Empire) against 'Ali's caliphate in order to garner sympathy for 'Uthman's caliphate and its 'unjust' ending. "[A messenger] came to the Syrians with the bloodstained shirt 'Uthman was wearing when he was killed, and with the severed fingers of Na'ilah, his wife—two with the knuckles and part of the palm, two cut off at the base, and half a thumb—Mu'awiyah hung the shirt on the *minbar*…the people kept on coming

---

[166] Ibid, 180.
[167] Ibid, 216.

and crying over it as it hung on the *minbar*, with the fingers attached to it, for a whole year."[168]

In some cases, women are also seen in al-Tabari's narrative playing the role of correcting their husbands' behaviors in order to uphold their proper image of modesty—a feminine trait endeared by Abbasid gender culture. When the second caliph, 'Umar ibn al-Khattab, asked his wife Umm Kulthum to join him for dinner one day, she pointed out that he was at fault for asking her such a question, for he knew she was not dressed for such an occasion. It was her husband's role, she advised, to ensure that she was properly dressed before meeting any strange men.[169] 'Umar then told her, "Is it not enough for you that you are called Umm Kulthum, daughter of 'Ali ibn Abi Talib and wife of the Commander of the Faithful, 'Umar?!" Despite her husband's request, Umm Kulthum still refused to join the company of a strange man.[170] Here al-Tabari's representation seems to commend the behavior of the wife, who corrects the husband, even if he is the caliph, and who upholds the gender ideal of female modesty upheld in Abbasid normative culture.

It should be noted, however, that although al-Tabari details examples of women acting as advisors in his Madina accounts, such a role does not seem to be a privilege handed to women in general. Based on his narrative, this role was assigned only to some select women, who appear to gain the trust of a male figure. It is also worth mentioning that it was not a role reserved solely for elite wives either. While all of the

---

[168]Al-Tabari, *The History of al-Tabari: Volume XVI The Community Divided, 196-197.*

[169] Al- Tabari, *The History of al-Tabari Volume: XIV The Conquest of Iran,* trans by G. Rex Smith (Albany: State University of New York Press, 1994), 85.

[170] Al- Tabari, *The History of al-Tabari Volume: XIV The Conquest of Iran,* 86.

aforementioned examples represent elite women, al-Tabari also specifies the cases of anonymous women advising their family members on the correct course of action. For example, during the wars between the Quraysh and the Muslim community, al-Tabari tells us about a man who for years abandoned his family and eventually returned to his sister. After she berated him for his behavior of leaving his family, he asked her for advice on how to go forward and whether or not he should ally with the Prophet. She responded, "By God, I think that you should join him forthwith, for if the man is a prophet, then the one who joins him first will have an exquisite virtue; and if he is a king you will not be humbled in the glory of the Yemen, you being what you are." The brother believed this was a good advice and immediately joined the Prophet,[171] which from al-Tabari's viewpoint placed him in a more virtuous path, and which in turn validates the good advisory role women played in men's lives.

Whereas in the next chapter we will see how al-Tabari found fault with feminine expression of emotionality in the public sphere, in this chapter we have seen that under certain restrictions some women are represented as rational thinkers and good advisors, a role they are allowed to play without contesting or threatening the authority and power of men as prescribed in the gender norms of al-Tabari's culture. In such portrayals it can be argued that he is adhering to the normative gender roles, honoring the women advisors who upheld the position of obedience to men's authority.

---

[171] Al-Tabari, *The History of al-Tabari Volume: IX The Last Years of the Prophet,* trans by Ismail K. Poonawala (Albany: State University of New York Press, 1990), 66.

Chapter Seven

Al-Tabari's Portrayal of Women as Emotional Players through

Mourning the Dead

Commenting on the hegemonic gender discourse in the Western intellectual tradition,

Alison M. Jaggar states:

> Emotions usually have been considered as potentially or actually subversive of knowledge. From Plato until the present, with a few notable exceptions, reason rather than emotion has been regarded as the indispensable faculty for acquiring knowledge. Typically, although again not invariable, the rational has been contrasted with the emotional, and this contrasted pair then often have been linked with other dichotomies. Not only has reason been contrasted with emotion, but it has also been associated with the mental, the cultural, the universal, the public and the male, whereas emotion has been associated with the irrational, the physical, the natural, and, of course, the female. [172]

Following a similar gender rationale, al-Tabari's seems to hold that there is an innate

difference between men and women, demonstrating women to be the far more emotional

gender in relation to men who are supposedly more rational and therefore deserve to hold

the authority of leadership. Depiction of women's emotionality abounds, not only in al-

Tabari's historical narrative, but also in many other Abbasid accounts of the Madina

period. While in the previous chapter it was shown how in al-Tabari narrative several

cases of women demonstrate their capacity of making wise decisions in matters regarding

---

[172] Alison M. Jaggar, "Love and Knowledge: Emotion in Feminist Epistemology," in *Feminist Social Thought: A Reader*, ed by Diana Tietjens Meyers (New York: Routledge, 1997), 284.

the public sphere, it is argued here that al-Tabari's strong focus on feminine

emotionality cautions against women being the final decision makers in either family or

community matters. For it is possible, as some of al-Tabari's accounts demonstrate,

when women act independently of men's authority, that their true emotional nature could

dominate and could lead in turn to negative result, as the case was with 'Aisha's role in

the Battle of the Camel.

A primary way al-Tabari's narrative demonstrates the emotional nature of women

is his description of such emotionality in their expression of grief. In these account, al-

Tabari's depiction of women's expression of grief far exceeds that of men, thus

representing women as the more emotional, and therefore the less rational sex. Al-Tabari

distaste of excessive emotional grief can be seen most clearly in his passages regarding

the Prophet's teaching on this matter. In one passage, for example, the Prophet is

reported to have always restrained his expression of grief:

> 'Alqamah asked ['A'isha], "Mother [of the Faithful], how did the
> Messenger of God behave?" She replied: "His eye did not weep for
> anyone. When his grief for someone became intense or when he was
> upset, he would only take hold of his beard."[173]

In another passage, the Prophet is reported to have been unnerved by a grieving woman,

as he was choosing between her and another woman for a wife:

> After the Messenger of God conquered al-Qamus, the fortress of Ibn Abi
> al-Huqayq, Safiyyah bt. Huyayy b. Akhtab was brought to him, and
> another woman with her. Bilal, who was the one who brought them, led
> them past some of the slain Jews. When the woman who was with
> Safiyyah saw them, she cried out, struck her face, and poured dust on her

---

[173] Al-Tabari, *The History of al-Tabari: Volume VIII The Victory of Islam,* 40.

head. When the Messenger of God saw her, he said, "Take this she-devil away
from me!" He commanded that Safiyyah should be kept behind him and
that his cloak should be cast over her. Thus the Muslims knew that the
Messenger of God had chosen her for himself.[174]

In this passage one can see that the Prophet gave preference to the woman who did not

express strong grief when seeing the slain bodies, choosing the less emotional woman to

be his new wife. The idea that women have a weaker emotional nature can be seen also

in al-Tabari's selection of reports in the aftermath of the Battle of the Camel. Once 'Ali

ibn Talib won the battle, he went to 'A'isha's house to confront her. While mourning the

deaths of the fallen soldiers, a woman sitting on 'A'isha's porch lashed out at the caliph

as he walked by. "'Ali! Killer of loved ones! Splitter of groups! May Allah make your

sons fatherless, as you have done to the sons of 'Abdallah!" [175] To this, al-Tabari reports,

'Ali acted in a reserved manner and did not respond to her. Later, when his followers

expressed anger at the woman's disrespect, he remarked:

> Don't any of you dishonor women! Don't force your way into any house!
> Don't stir up discord with any women by hurting her, even if they shout
> abuse at your women-folk and call your leaders and your honest men
> fools. They are weak. We have been commanded to hold back from
> them…A man who recompenses a woman by beating her will have his
> descendants after him reproached for it. So let me not hear of anyone that
> he has confronted a woman. I will punish him as the most wicked of
> people.[176]

Although the command not to hurt women may be commendable and certainly puts 'Ali

in a more positive light as a good Muslim, in gender terms, the implication of al-Tabari's

report seems to say that women hold less responsibility for their words and actions

---

[174] Al-Tabari, *The History of al-Tabari: Volume VIII The Victory of Islam, 122.*
[175] Al-Tabari, *The History of al-Tabari: Volume XVI The Community Divided,* 165.
[176] Al-Tabari, *The History of al-Tabari: Volume XVI The Community Divided,* 165.

because they have less control over their reactions and are more dominated by their

emotions, and therefore are considered weak. Al-Tabari's narrative demonstrates the true

manliness of 'Ali, in contrast to the weakness of women, for he can control his reactions,

while the woman could not. Furthermore, 'Ali is depicted as a man of true manliness

because he acts as the protector of women despite their display of negative emotions

towards him.

Throughout our narrative men and women's reaction to tragedy are contrasted,

often showing men responding, in contrast to women, in a more thoughtful and collected

manner. This can be seen in the account depicting the aftermath of the death of the

Prophet. Because of the significance of this event, al-Tabari includes an account of both

female and male reactions. However, regarding the death of other figures in the Madina

Muslim community our historian does not give account of the men's reactions, focusing

more on the women's reactions. The one man whom al-Tabari reports to have publicly

grieved after the death of the Prophet was his successor, Abu Bakr. There is, however, a

strong distinction between Abu Bakr's reaction and that of women who mourned the

Prophet's death. After hearing the news of the Prophet's death, al-Tabari records in a

more detailed fashion the outward mourning of his wives and female relatives. In this

account, 'A'isha says, "[I] got up beating my chest and slapping my face along with the

women."[177] While this is most likely a cultural tradition prevalent in the gendered culture

of the Arabian peninsula, one that permits women to give vent to their grief in public, the

same tradition frowns upon men who show a public expression of their grief, for it might

---

[177] Al- Tabari, *The History of al-Tabari Volume: IX The Last Years of the Prophet,* trans by Ismail K. Poonawala (Albany: State University of New York Press, 1990), 183.

taint their normative image of a strong masculinity. Accordingly, al-Tabari's account depicts women expressing their emotional outburst of grief, but it refrains from the inclusion of men's expression of grief. Thus Abu Bakr's reaction to the death of the Prophet is perceived in the same account as a thoughtful and controlled reaction, in contrast to the emotional reaction of women. Al-Tabari does not show him to demonstrate any outward signs of emotion, Abu Bakr respectfully goes to the Prophet's body and whispers, "With my father may you be ransomed, and with my mother! Indeed, you have tasted the death, which God had decreed you. No [other] death will ever overtake you."[178]

A similar account, focusing on women's expression of emotional mourning can be seen in al-Tabari's narrative following the deaths of the four succeeding caliphs. For example, after the death of Abu Bakr, and despite the new caliph 'Umar ibn al-Khattab's orders, Abu Bakr's female family members refused to stop weeping:

> 'A'isha carried out the mourning for him. 'Umar b. al-Khattab
> approached until he stood at the door. He forbade the women to weep for
> Abu Bakr, but they refused to stop. 'Umar said to Hisham b. al-Walid,
> "Go inside and bring me the daughter of Abu Quhafah, the sister of Abu
> Bakr." When she heard that from 'Umar, 'A'isha said to Hisham, "I
> forbid my house to you." But 'Umar said to Hisham, "Go on in, for I have
> given you permission." Thus, Hisham entered and brought out Umm
> Farwah, the sister of Abu Bakr, to 'Umar, who raised his whip over her
> and gave her a number of blows. The weeping women scattered when
> they heard that.[179]

---

[178] Al- Tabari, *The History of al-Tabari Volume: IX The Last Years of the Prophet,* 184.

[179] Al- Tabari, *The History of al-Tabari Volume: XI The Challenges to the Empires,* trans by Khalid Yahya Blankinship (Albany: State University of New York Press, 1993), 137-138.

As can be seen in this passage the female reaction to death far exceeds the male reaction, which is not even noted by al-Tabari on this occasion. Further, one can also see that men in authority are not only represented to be in control of their own emotions, and therefore stronger, but more importantly, they are represented as the controllers of women's emotions as well.

While sometimes al-Tabari makes excuses for women to act in an emotional manner, like in the aftermath of a war or a family death, at other times he highlights women's erratic, and needless, emotional show of grief. For example, after the Battle of Badr the Qurashi leaders decided not to mourn for their dead for fear that it would bring joy to Muhammad and his Companions if they heard it.

> Al-Aswad b. al-Muttalib had lost three sons, Zam'ah b.al-Aswad, Aqil b. al-Aswad, and al-Harith b. al-Aswad, and he wanted to weep for them. While he was in this condition, he suddenly heard a woman wailing in the night. He said to his slave, as he himself had lost his sight, "See if wailing has been made lawful and whether Quraysh are weeping for their dead, so that perhaps I can weep for Abu Hakimah (meaning Zam'ah), for my belly is on fire." When the slave came back he said, "It is only a woman weaping for a camel of hers which she has lost." It was on that occasion that he composed the following verse:
>
> Does she weep because a camel of hers is lost, and does sleeplessness prevent her from sleeping?
> Do not weep for a young camel, but for Badr where our good fortune deserted us,
> For Badr and the chiefs of the Banu Husays, and Makhzum and the clan of Abu al-Walid.
> And weep, if you must weep, for 'Aqil, and weep for al-Harith, the lion of lions,
> Weep for them without tiring, and there is no equal to Abu Hakimah.[180]

---

[180] Al- Tabari, *The History of al-Tabari Volume: VII The Foundation of the Community*, 70.

In this narrative we can see how al-Aswad is able to restrain himself from displaying his grief over the death of his three sons, and how an unnamed woman cannot control herself over a much more trivial matter. Although one has to admit that loss of the camel may have meant for this woman loss of her livelihood.

Although al-Tabari at times seems to be apprehensive of women's over-emotional reactions to tragedy, his accounts of other incidents of death demonstrate that such female emotions are acceptable from women, but not from men. This is illustrated when, after hearing the lamentation of women over the death of other soldiers, the Prophet became upset and said, "But Hamzah has no woman weeping for him." Following this, "Sa'd b. Mu'adh and Usayd b. Hudayr came back to the settlement of the Banu 'Abd al-Ashhal, and told their women to gird themselves up and to go and weep for the Messenger of God's uncle."[181] This account demonstrates that women because they are assigned the weaker gender role are expected to show their weaknesses more openly than men, because they are supposed to demonstrate strength and control of their emotions on such occasions.

As shown in the previous chapters, as well as in this one, the historical narrative has proven to be an important tool in defining the gender dichotomy of the period in which it was written. This is equally true of al-Tabari's historical representation of women of the Madina period. As Barbara Stowasser explains, "The 'images' as recorded/transmitted by medieval scholars of Islam provided both the paradigm for the

---

[181] Al-Tabari, *The History of al-Tabari Volume: VII The Foundation of the Community,* 137.

limits that needed to be placed on women's roles in religion and society, and also their

justification, that is, scripturally proof of 'woman's nature'."[182]

---

[182] Stowasser, 106.

Chapter Eight

Concluding Remarks

One could argue that with each century a new type of historical interpretation emerges, for within each century new questions are found to be more prevalent depending on the interests and conflicts a society is experiencing. As argued before history can prove to be a powerful tool in constructing and enforcing certain features of cultural conditioning. It can support the assumption of the biological basis for gender roles, for instance, traditional thinkers, like al-Tabari, subscribed to the notion that women are the child-rearers and men are the providers for a family, because of their inherent biological natures. This as well as other gender assumptions can be inferred from al-Tabari's text. In the discipline of medieval Arab Muslim historiography, al-Tabari is considered as one of the most influential figures. His historical narrative set a standard for later historians for centuries to come, and it may be argued that his views on gender were more or less shared by other male historians of his period as well.

This thesis has argued that al-Tabari projected his own cultural concepts of gender onto his representation of the women of the Madina period. As was shown, he promoted his gender beliefs in a number of ways. First of all, one can see this through his selection of historical events, which generally under-represents the role of women. This is not only typical of al-Tabari's history, but like other male-authored historical accounts, women seem to be more or less invisible in the course of history. Secondly, when women do appear in his history they are usually represented in such a way that either praises or shames them in accordance to the predominant gender norms of the historian's culture. While al-Tabari rarely makes direct comments on his historical reports, it may be argued that he indirectly expresses his own views and assumptions through referencing the opinions of historical figures that act or comment during the reported events. Thirdly, as has been shown in the case of 'A'isha and the rebellious women, and their assumption of leading political roles, we find that al-Tabari seems to focus on how such political involvement may lead to negative results because of an assumed belief in the emotional and weak nature of women. Not surprisingly, such a view coincides with al-Tabari's gender assumption that women should not hold positions of power or authority in the public sphere. While al-Tabari's ideal image of the proper Muslim woman may have been contested in practice, as is shown in 'Aisha's case, I am arguing that al-Tabari through his historical narrative wished to prescribe for women an idealized image of the good Muslim woman which they should not transgress.

This thesis mainly focused on the gender assumptions al-Tabari projected on women during the Madina period, however, it would be interesting if other studies may examine other periods in al-Tabari's text in order to show how his historical narrative informs and is informed by the construction of prevailing cultural gender norms. Another interesting line of study would be to compare different historians' perspectives of the image of women of the Madina period. Furthermore, one could analyze the gender norms al-Tabari projected onto the men of the Madina period, for while he tried to construct an image of the ideal Muslim woman in this period, it could also be argued

that he did the same for men.

www.ingramcontent.com/pod-product-compliance
Lightning Source LLC
LaVergne TN
LVHW051308200726

843510LV00010B/1324